THE ISLAMIC WORLD
AND THE WEST
A.D. 622–1492

MAJOR ISSUES IN HISTORY

Editor

C. WARREN HOLLISTER

University of California, Santa Barbara

William F. Church: *The Impact of Absolutism in France: National Experience under Richelieu, Mazarin, and Louis XIV*
Robert O. Collins: *The Partition of Africa: Illusion or Necessity*
J. B. Conacher: *The Emergence of Parliamentary Democracy in Britain in the Nineteenth Century*
Gerald D. Feldman: *German War Aims, 1914-1918: The Development of an Historical Debate*
Frank J. Frost: *Democracy and the Athenians*
Paul Hauben: *The Spanish Inquisition*
Bennett D. Hill: *Church and State in the Middle Ages*
Boyd H. Hill: *The Rise of the First Reich: Germany in the Tenth Century*
C. Warren Hollister: *The Impact of the Norman Conquest*
C. Warren Hollister: *The Twelfth-Century Renaissance*
Thomas M. Jones: *The Becket Controversy*
Tom B. Jones: *The Sumerian Problem*
Jeffry Kaplow: *France on the Eve of Revolution*
Archibald Lewis: *Islamic World and the West*
Anthony Molho: *Social and Economic Foundations of the Italian Renaissance*
E. W. Monter: *European Witchcraft*
Donald Queller: *The Latin Conquest of Constantinople*
Joachim Remak: *The First World War: Causes, Conduct, Consequences*
Jeffrey Russell: *Medieval Religious Dissent*
Max Salvadori: *European Liberalism*
Arthur J. Slavin: *Humanism, Reform, and Reformation*
W. Warren Wagar: *The Idea of Progress Since the Renaissance*
Bertie Wilkinson: *The Creation of the Medieval Parliament*
L. Pearce Williams: *Relativity Theory: Its Origins and Impact on Modern Thought*
Roger L. Williams: *The Commune of Paris, 1871*

THE ISLAMIC WORLD AND THE WEST

A.D. 622–1492

EDITED BY

Archibald R. Lewis

John Wiley & Sons, Inc.
New York · London · Sydney · Toronto

*To My Friends in
Beirut, Cairo, Istanbul and Teheran*

Copyright © 1970, by John Wiley & Sons, Inc.

All rights reserved. No part of this book may be reproduced by any means, nor transmitted, nor translated into a machine language without the written permission of the publisher.

Library of Congress Catalogue Card Number: 76-126229

Cloth: ISBN 0-471-53200-2   Paper: ISBN 0-471-53201-0

Printed in the United States of America

PREFACE

Thoughtful individuals, surveying the contemporary age in which we live, cannot fail to grasp the importance of the numerous relationships that link the Western and Islamic worlds and that may well determine the way the future unfolds. These relationships are not solely the result of recent contacts between the two civilizations. They have a long history in the course of which the medieval centuries between the flight of Mohammed to Medina in A.D. 622 and the fall of Granada in A.D. 1492 have a particular importance. It was during these years that a great portion of the present attitudes of Moslems toward Western European civilization (and vice versa) were formed.

We can now speak of each of these civilizations in medieval times with a great deal more assurance than once was the case. During recent decades, scholars have slowly made clear to us the way that medieval Western Christendom developed and how its political, social, religious, economic, and cultural life functioned. And, although a great deal still remains to be understood concerning the world of medieval Islam, so much progress has been made in the scholarship of recent years that we can, at last, chart the major outlines of its development. All of this scholarship, properly understood, can reveal to us some of the basic reasons why these two civilizations, possessing so much in common, had by the late fifteenth century become hostile to one another. This book attempts to explain this estrangement.

As the reader examines the original sources and secondary accounts that make up this volume, he should grasp a few preliminary points. The first of these is an understanding of how differently the Western European and Islamic worlds developed during the Middle Ages. In general, Western Europe's development is well known. It began with a slow, steady, painful change from the late Roman World, which collapsed in the wake of barbarian invasions, until the late tenth and early eleventh centuries. This formative era is known as the Early Middle Ages. It was followed by a period of rich development during the eleventh, twelfth, and thirteenth centuries, called the High Middle Ages, an era characterized by Gothic cathedrals, Papal authority, Crusaders, and the rise of towns, universities, and parliaments. It ended with a period of difficult readjustment—the Later Middle Ages or Early Renaissance—which led to the more modern world of the Reformation, the Scientific Revolution, geographic discovery, and overseas expansion.

In contrast to this pattern of development, the Moslem world had only a brief and explosive formative period of growth during the seventh and eighth centuries, when its victorious armies carried its distinctive religion and its Arabic tongue to lands stretching from India and China to the Atlantic. This was followed by a flowering of its civilization between the ninth and late twelfth centuries in cities like Baghdad, Bokhara, Isfahan, Cairo, and Cordova. This flowering was followed by a thirteenth-century decline, which was marked especially by a great Mongol invasion of the Middle East. The decline was not a temporary phenomenon, as was the case with Western Europe in the fourteenth and fifteenth centuries. Instead, for most of the Moslem world, it continued to relatively recent times. Thus, each civilization followed a somewhat different rhythm of development, which we must remember as we examine their effect on one another.

Second, we must remind ourselves constantly of the importance that each of these civilizations attached to religion. Both regarded it as, by far, the most important element in life; God seemed very close, and it was man's duty to serve Him in ways that the Church and Mohammed, respectively, had outlined for their followers.

That does not mean that the religious life of either the Western Christian or the Islamic worlds was fixed or unchanging. Nothing could be further from the truth. Western Christendom's faith and religious institutions changed in many ways between the Patristic age and that of the Popes and Councils of the Later Middle Ages, while the Islamic World moved from a simple belief in Koran and Hadiths, or *traditions* associated with Mohammed, or Moslem Law, through an intellectualized faith, to the fully developed world of the *Sharia*, and mysticism of the thirteenth and fourteenth centuries.

What is important, however, is not that many changes took place in religious life, but that both Western Europeans and Moslems alike tended to regard their faith as of overwhelming importance—more vital to them than political, economic, and social matters, or the intellectual, artistic, or literary culture that they enjoyed. This attitude, so different from that of the present day, is a facet of these civilizations during medieval times that we should not forget.

Third, we must remember that during most of this period, Western European civilization was definitely inferior to Moslem civilization and was, in comparison to it, underdeveloped. This is the reason that the average upper-class Moslem felt superior to most Western Europeans, whether they were merchants, warriors, scholars, or priests. This sense of superiority continued even after the thirteenth century when Western Europe had caught up to the Islamic World's level of development. It helps to explain why, for centuries, Western Europeans were eager to copy many facets of Moslem culture, and why Moslems, except in military matters, were too little aware of European progress and accomplishments.

Thus, when we examine contacts between a changing Western Christendom and a developing Islamic World during these medieval centuries, we should keep in mind the very different rhythm of each civilization, the overriding importance that each attached to its system of religious beliefs and practices, and the fact that during most of the period the civilization of Islam was more sophisticated than that of the Latin West. It is against the background of these basic realities that a tragedy of misunderstanding, estrangement, and hostility eventually emerged out of the meeting and mingling of their varied ways of life.

Archibald Lewis

University of Massachusettes at Amherst

SERIES PREFACE

The reading program in a history survey course traditionally has consisted of a large two-volume textbook and, perhaps, a book of readings. This simple reading program requires few decisions and little imagination on the instructor's part, and tends to encourage in the student the virtue of careful memorization. Such programs are by no means things of the past, but they certainly do not represent the wave of the future.

The reading program in survey courses at many colleges and universities today is far more complex. At the risk of over-simplification, and allowing for many exceptions and overlaps, it can be divided into four categories: (1) textbook, (2) original source readings, (3) specialized historical essays and interpretive studies, and (4) historical problems.

After obtaining an overview of the course subject matter (textbook), sampling the original sources, and being exposed to selective examples of excellent modern historical writing (historical essays), the student can turn to the crucial task of weighing various possible interpretations of major historical issues. It is at this point that memory gives way to creative critical thought. The "problems approach," in other words, is the intellectual climax of a thoughtfully conceived reading program and is, indeed, the most characteristic of all approaches to historical pedagogy among the newer generation of college and university teachers.

The historical problems books currently available are many and varied. Why add to this information explosion? Because the Wiley Major Issues Series constitutes an endeavor to produce something new that will respond to pedagogical needs thus far unmet. First, it is a series of individual volumes—one per problem. Many good teachers would much prefer to select their own historical issues rather than be tied to an inflexible sequence of issues imposed by a publisher and bound together between two covers. Second, the Wiley Major Issues Series is based on the idea of approaching the significant problems of history through a deft interweaving of primary sources and secondary analysis, fused together by the skill of a scholar-editor. It is felt that the essence of a historical issue cannot be satisfactorily probed either by placing a body of undigested source materials into the hands of inexperienced students or by limiting these students to the controversial literature of modern scholars who debate the meaning of sources the student never sees. This series approaches historical problems by exposing students to both the finest historical thinking on the issue and some of the evidence on which this thinking is based. This synthetic approach should prove far more fruitful than either the raw-source approach or the exclusively second-hand approach, for it combines the advantages—and avoids the serious disadvantages—of both.

Finally, the editors of the individual volumes in the Major Issues Series have been chosen from among the ablest scholars in their fields. Rather than faceless referees, they are historians who know their issues from the inside and, in most instances, have themselves contributed significantly to the relevant scholarly literature. It has been the editorial policy of this series to permit the editor-scholars of the individual volumes the widest possible latitude both in formulating their topics and in organizing their materials. Their scholarly competence has been unquestioningly respected; they have been encouraged to approach the problems as they see fit. The titles and themes of the series volumes have been suggested in nearly every case by the scholar-editors themselves. The criteria have been (1) that the issue be of relevance to undergraduate lecture courses in history, and (2) that it be an issue which the scholar-editor knows thoroughly and in which he has done creative work. And, in general, the second criterion has been given precedence over the first. In short, the question "What are the significant historical issues today?" has been answered not by general editors or sales departments but by the scholar-teachers who are responsible for these volumes.

University of California,   *C. Warren Hollister*
Santa Barbara

CONTENTS

PART III

*Alienation and Divergence—From the End of the Crusading
States in Syria to the Fall of Granada,* A.D. *1291–1492*

THE ISLAMIC WORLD
AND THE WEST
A.D. 622–1492

PART ONE

Ignorance and Discovery—From the Hegira to the First Crusade, A.D. 622—1095

The period of almost half a millennium, stretching from the Hegira to the launching of the First Crusade, marks the formative period in relations between the Islamic World and the West. It was during these years that we can see the beginning of a conflict between these two civilizations—based upon their religious difference. These differences are outlined in statements found in the Koran which deal with Jesus and his religious significance (Selection 1). These passages show that Mohammed respected Jesus as the greatest prophet before his own coming and explain why he enjoined his followers to treat with tolerance those Christians who submitted to Islamic rule. But they also reveal an attitude which was completely unacceptable to Western Christians and which, by the mid-ninth century, had caused a violent ideological clash between Christians and Moslems in Islamic Spain (Selection 2)—one that gave a foretaste of the future.

However, the major aspect of these years does not lie in toleration or clashes between Moslems and Western Christians, but rather in their mutual ignorance and isolation. These came about in large measure because the Byzantine world lay as a barrier between the two civilizations. Thus, despite a contiguous frontier in Spain, despite fairly regular Christian pilgrimages to the Holy Land, and despite an occasional exchange of diplomatic missions—especially at the time of Charlemagne and Louis the Pious— Western civilization and Islam remained culturally and politically estranged. Even in an economic sense, many of the more useful contracts resulted from the travels of the ubiquitous Rhademite Jews (Selection 5).

1

Then, in the mid-ninth century, Islamic naval attacks launched by Moslem Spaniards and North Africans led to the conquest of the Mediterranean islands. The resulting Moslem control over the Balearics, Sardinia, Corsica, Sicily, Crete, and Cyprus, and over some mainland bases to the north as well, destroyed Byzantine naval strength and brought Western European and the Moslems face to face in a new way (Selection 4). At about the same time, adventurous Scandinavian merchants began to trade with Moslem traffickers on the lower Volga (Selection 3). These developments led not only to violent military contracts but also to intensified economic relationships via Spain, Russia, and Italian cities such as Naples, Amalfi, and Venice (Selection 5).

There was much less knowledge and intercourse with the Islamic world in the interior of Western Europe where the new feudalistic society of Northern France was beginning to emerge as a powerful force. Nor was this ignorance to change until large armies of Northern Christians began to cross the Pyrenees into Spain to take part in the conquest of Sicily and to journey into Syria on the First Crusade.

1 TRANSLATED AND ARRANGED BY

George M. Lamsa

SELECTIONS FROM THE KORAN CONCERNING JESUS AND CHRISTIANITY

These selections provide much of the basis for later agreements and disagreements between Islam and Christianity. Islam, of course, was regarded in the West at first as a Christian heresy, while the passages which follow make it clear that Mohammed, who obviously received his knowledge of Christianity via an oral tradition, had a great respect for Jesus. Mohammed seems to have accepted the virgin birth of Jesus and to have viewed Him as especially favored of God and even as a special judge at the Last Judgment. On the other hand, he obviously believed Jesus to be only a prophet, and therefore he rejected the concept of the Trinity. Mohammed was also, in general, somewhat hostile to the organized Church and monasticism. He seems convinced that the Crucifixion should be interpreted in a Gnostic or Monophysite way, that is, that Jesus was essentially a spiritual being who only appeared to die on the Cross. It is easy, therefore, to see in these passages why Mohammedans came to tolerate Christians as followers of Jesus but, on the other hand, why Christians could not accept Mohammed's views concerning their faith.

SOURCE. George M. Lamsa, *The Short Koran* (Englewood Cliffs, New Jersey: Prentice-Hall, Inc., 1949), pp. 145–162. Reprinted by permission of the publisher.

VIRGIN MARY AND JESUS

Sura 3 : 35

Remember when the wife of Imran said, O my Lord! verily I have vowed unto Thee that which is in my womb, to be dedicated to Thy service: accept it therefore of me; for Thou art He who heareth and knoweth.

And when she was delivered of it, she said, O my Lord! verily I have brought forth a female child! and God well knew what she had brought forth and a male is not as a female: I have called her Mary; and I commend her to Thy protection, and also her issue, against Satan driven away with stones.

Therefore the Lord accepted her with a gracious acceptance, and caused her to be reared in excellency. And Zacharias took care of her; whenever Zacharias went into her chamber, he found provisions with her: and he said, O Mary! whence hadst thou this? she answered, This is from God; for God provideth for whom He pleaseth without measure.

There did Zacharias pray to his Lord, and said, O my Lord! give me from Thee a good offspring, for Thou art the hearer of prayer.

And the angels called to him, while he stood praying in the chamber, saying, Verily God promiseth thee a son named John, who shall bear witness to the Word which cometh from God; an honorable person, chaste, and one of the righteous prophets.

He said, O my Lord! how shall I have a son, when old age hath overtaken me, and my wife is barren? The angel said, So God doth that which He pleaseth.

Zacharias answered, O my Lord! give me a sign. The angel said, thy sign shall be that thou shalt speak unto no man for three days, otherwise than by gesture: remember thy Lord often, and praise Him evening and morning.

And remember when the angels said, O Mary! verily God hath chosen thee, and hath purified thee, and hath chosen thee above all the women of the world:

O Mary! be devout towards thy Lord, and worship and bow down with those who bow down.

This is a part of the secret history which God revealeth unto thee O Mohammed! although thou wast not present with them when they threw in their reeds to cast lots as which of them should rear

Mary, neither wast thou with them, when they disputed among themselves about her.

And remember when the angels said, O Mary! verily God sendeth thee good tidings of the Word from Himself; his name shall be Christ Jesus, the son of Mary, honorable in this world and in the world to come, and one of those who approach near to the presence of God.

And he shall speak unto people in the cradle, and when he is grown up; and he shall be one of the righteous:

She said, O my Lord! how shall I have a son when no man hath touched me? The angel said, So God createth that which He pleaseth: when He decreeth a thing, He only saith unto it, Be, and it is:

God shall teach him the Scripture and Wisdom, and the Law, and the Gospel; and shall appoint him His Apostle to the children of Israel; and he shall say, Verily I have come unto you with a sign from your Lord; for I will make before you, of clay, as it were the figure of a bird; then I will breathe into it, and it shall become a bird by permission of God; and I will heal those that hath been blind, and the leper, and I will raise the dead by the permission of God; and I will prophesy unto you what ye eat, and what ye lay up for store in your houses. Verily herein will be a sign unto you, if ye believe.

And I have come to confirm the Law which was revealed before me, and to allow unto you as lawful, part of that which hath been forbidden you: and I have come unto you with a sign from your Lord; therefore fear God, and obey me.

Verily God is my Lord, and you Lord: therefore serve Him. This is the right way.

But when Jesus perceived their unbelief, he said, Who will be my helpers in the work of God? The apostles said, We will be the helpers in the work of God; we believe in God and do thou bear witness that we are true believers.

O our Lord! we believe in that which Thou hast sent down, and we have followed the apostle; write us down therefore with those who bear witness of him.

And the Jews devised a plot against him; but God devised a plot against them; and God is the best deviser of plots.

And remember when God said, O Jesus! verily I will cause thee to die, and I will take thee up unto Me, and I will deliver thee from the unbelievers; and I will place those who follow thee above the unbelievers, until the day of Resurrection: then unto Me shall ye return, and I will judge between you of that concerning which ye disagree.

Moreover, as for the infidels, I will punish them with a grievous punishment in this world, and in that which is to come; and there shall be none to help them.

But as for those who believe, and do that which is right, He shall give them their reward; for God loveth not the wicked doers.

These signs and this prudent admonition doth God rehearse unto thee.

Verily the likeness of Jesus in the sight of God is as the likeness of Adam: He created him out of the dust, and then said unto him, Be; and he was.

This is the truth from thy Lord; be not therefore one of those who doubt.

And whoever shall dispute with thee concerning him, after the knowledge which hath been given thee, say unto them, Come, let us call together our sons, and your sons, and our wives, and your wives, and ourselves and yourselves; then let us make imprecations, and invoke the curse of God on those who lie.

Sura 66 : 12

Mary the daughter of Imran; who preserved her chastity; and into whose womb God breathed of His spirit, and who believed in the words of her Lord and His Scriptures, was a devout and obedient person.

THE BIRTH OF JESUS CHRIST

Sura 19 : 16

Make mention in the Book of the Koran the story of Mary; when she retired from her family to a place towards the east, and took a veil to conceal herself from them; and God sent His spirit Gabriel unto her, and he appeared unto her in the likeness of a perfect man.

She said, I fly for refuge unto the Merciful God, that He may defend me from thee: If thou fearest Him, thou wilt not approach me.

He answered, Verily, I am the messenger of thy Lord, and am sent to give thee a holy son.

She said, how shall I have a son, seeing a man hath not touched me, and I am no harlot?

Gabriel replied, So shall it be; thy Lord hath saith, This is easy with Me; and We will perform it, that We may obtain him for a sign unto men, and a mercy from Us: for it is a thing which is decreed.

So she conceived him: and she retired aside with him to a distant place.

And the pains of childbirth came upon her near the trunk of a palm-tree. She said, Would to God I had died before this, and become a thing forgotten and lost in oblivion!

And he who was beneath her called to her saying, Be not grieved, for thy Lord hath provided a rivulet under thee;

And shake the trunk of the palm tree, and it shall let fall ripe dates upon thee, ready gathered.

Eat and drink, and calm thy mind. Moreover, if thou see any man and he questions thee, say, Verily I have vowed a fast unto the Merciful; wherefore I will by no means speak to a man this day.

So she brought the child to her people, carrying him in her arms. And they said unto her, O Mary: now hast thou done a strange thing!

O sister of Aaron! thy father was not a bad man, neither was thy mother a harlot.

But she made signs unto the babe to answer them; and they said, How shall we speak to him, who is an infant in the cradle?

Whereupon the babe said, Verily I am the servant of God; He hath given me the Book of the Gospel, and hath appointed me a prophet:

And He hath made me blessed, wheresoever I shall be; and hath commanded me to observe prayer, and to give alms, so long as I shall live;

And He hath made me dutiful towards my mother, and hath not made me proud, or unhappy.

And peace is on me the day I was born, and the day that I shall die, and the day whereon I shall be raised to life.

This is Jesus, the Son of Mary; the Word of truth, concerning whom they doubt.

It is not meet for God that He should beget a son: God forbid! When He decreeth a thing, He only saith unto it, Be, and it is.

And verily God is my Lord, and your Lord; wherefore serve Him: this is the right way.

. . . . .

JESUS IS NOT GOD

Sura 5 : 75

They do blaspheme who say, Verily God is Christ the son of Mary; since Christ said, O children of Israel! worship God, my Lord and your God shall exclude him from Paradise, and his habitation shall be hell fire; and the ungodly shall have none to help them.

They certainly do blaspheme who say, God is the third of three, for there is no God besides one God; and if they refrain not from what they say, a painful torment shall surely be inflicted on such of them as are blasphemers.

Will they not therefore be turned unto God, and ask pardon of Him? since God is Gracious and Merciful.

Christ the son of Mary is no more than an apostle; other apostles have preceded him; and his mother was a righteous woman: they both ate food. Behold! how God doth declare unto them His signs! and then behold! how they turn aside from the truth!

Say unto them, Will ye worship, besides God, that which can cause you neither harm nor profit? But God, He it is Who heareth and knoweth.

Say, O ye who have received the Scriptures! exceed not the just bounds in your religion, by speaking beside the truth; neither follow the desires of people who have heretofore erred, and who have misled many, and have gone astray from the straight path.

. . . . .

Sura 5 : 112

On a certain day will God assemble the apostles, and will say unto them, What answer was returned you, when ye preached unto the people to whom ye were sent? They shall say, We have no knowledge, but Thou art the Knower of Secrets.

When God shall say, O Jesus, son of Mary! remember My favor towards thee, and towards thy mother: when I strengthen thee with the Holy Spirit, that thou shouldest speak unto men in the cradle, and when thou wast grown up, and when I taught thee the Scripture and Wisdom and the Law and the Gospel; and when thou didst create of clay as it were the figure of a bird, by My permission, and didst breathe into it, and it became a bird by My permission; and thou didst heal one blind from his birth, and the lepers, by My permission; and when thou didst bring forth the death from their graves, by My permission; and when I withheld the children of Israel from killing thee; when thou hadst come unto them with evident miracles, and such of them as believed not, said, This is nothing but manifest sorcery.

. . . . .

And when God shall say O Jesus, son of Mary! hast thou said unto men, Take me and my mother for two gods, beside God? He shall say, Praise be unto Thee! it is not for me to say that which I ought not; If I had said so, Thou wouldst surely have known it: Thou knowest what is in me, but I know not what is in Thee, for Thou art the Knower of Secrets.

I have not spoken to them any other than what Thou didst command me; namely, Worship God, my Lord and your Lord: and I was a witness of their actions while I stayed among them; but since Thou hast taken me to Thyself, Thou hast been the watcher over them; for Thou art Witness of All Things.

. . . . .

JESUS IS AN APOSTLE

Sura 4 : 171

O ye who have received the scriptures! exceed not the just bounds in your religion, neither say of God any other than the truth. Verily Christ Jesus the son of Mary is the Apostle of God and His Word, which He conveyed into Mary, and a Spirit proceeding from Him. Believe therefore in God and His apostles, and say not, There are three Gods: forbear this; it will be better for you. For God is but one God. Far be it from Him that He should have a Son! unto Him belongeth whatsoever is in the heavens and on the earth; and God is a sufficient protector.

Christ doth not proudly disdain to be a servant of God; neither

do the angels who approach near to His presence; and whoso dis-
daineth His worship and is puffed up with pride, God will gather
them all to Himself on the last day.

Unto those who believe, and do that which is right, He shall give
their rewards, and shall superabundantly add unto them of His
liberality: but those who are disdainful and proud, He will punish
with a grievous punishment; and they shall not find any to protect
or to help them, besides God.

GOD IS NOT BORN

Sura 5 : 19

They blaspheme who say, Verily God is Christ the son of Mary.
Say unto them, And who could obtain anything from God to the
contrary, if He pleased to destroy Christ the son of Mary, his
mother, and all those who are on the earth? For unto God
belongeth the kingdom of the heaven and earth, and whatsoever is
contained between them; He createth what He pleaseth and God is
Almighty.

Sura 9 : 30

The Jews say, Ezra is a son of God: and the Christians say Christ
is a son of God. This is their saying in their mouths: they imitate
the saying of those who were unbelievers in former times. May God
fight against them. How are they led away from the truth!

They take their priests and their monks for their lords, and Christ
the son of Mary, besides God; although they are commanded to
worship one God only. There is no God but He; far be that from
Him what they associate with Him!

They seek to extinguish the light of God with their mouths; but
God willeth no other than to perfect His light, although the infidels
may detest it.

It is He who hath sent His Apostle with the guidance and true
religion: that He may cause it to appear superior to every other
religion; although the idolaters be averse thereto.

O true believers! verily many of the priests and monks devour the
substance of men in vanity and obstruct the way of God.

JEWS DID NOT KILL JESUS

Sura 4 : 156

They [Jews] have not believed on Jesus, and have spoken against Mary a grievous calumny, and have said, Verily, we have slain Christ Jesus son of Mary, the Apostle of God; yet they slew him not, neither crucified him, but he was represented by one in his likeness; and verily they who disagreed concerning him, were in a doubt as to this matter, and had no sure knowledge thereof, but followed only an uncertain opinion. They did not really kill him; but God took him up into Himself; and God is Mighty and Wise.

And there shall not be one of those who have received the Scriptures, who shall not believe in him, before his death, and on the day of Resurrection he shall be a witness against them.

2 FROM   *Edward P. Colbert*

THE MARTYRS OF CORDOVA

Between A.D. 850 and 859, in rather unusual fashion, a group of Spanish Christians of Cordova denounced Islam and Mohammed and, as a result, suffered martyrdom at the hands of the indignant Moslem officials and population of the city. Accounts of their martyrdom, written by Mozarab contemporaries Eulogius and Albar, have come down to us and are the basis of this account by Edward Colbert. These episodes are revealing because they illustrate exactly what many Christians thought of Islam in the Spain of the ninth century. They also serve as a warning that there were limits to the tolerance existing between Christians and Moslems, limits that were, in Spain, to lead in the future to outright persecution on both sides.

In a . . . paragraph . . . devoted to Perfectus, who was slain in April 850, Eulogius offers a brief sketch of Umaiyad wealth and power in Córdoba on the eve of the martyrdoms. "In the name of

SOURCE. Edward P. Colbert, *The Martyrs of Córdoba (850–859): A Study of the Sources* (Washington, D.C.: The Catholic University of America Press, 1962), pp. 194–203. Reprinted by permission of the publisher and the author.

the Lord. Our Lord Jesus Christ reigning in perpetuum, in the year of His Incarnation 850, Era 888, in the twenty-ninth year of the reign of Abd al-Rahman, in whose days the Arab people, having increased their possessions and authority in Spain, have occupied almost all Iberia with dire right. Córdoba, however, once called Patricia, now called the Royal City, because of his residence, has been exalted by him above all, elevated with honors, expanded in glory, piled full of riches, and with great energy filled with an abundance of all the delights of the world, more than one can believe or express. So much so that in every worldly pomp he exceeds, surpasses, and excels the preceding kings of his race. And meanwhile the church of the orthodox groans beneath his most grievous yoke and is beaten to destruction."

Eulogius then treats of the first martyr. The priest Perfectus was born in Córdoba and educated at the Basilica of St. Acisclus, where he spent most of his manhood. His rather good education, consisting of ecclesiastical training, letters, and some Arabic, deserves as much attention as Albar's complaint about the indifference of the laity towards ecclesiastical Latin culture. . . .

Perfectus was stopped one day on the streets of Córdoba by Moslems and asked to explain the Catholic faith and what he thought about Christ and Mohammed. Immediately, says Eulogius, he proclaimed that Christ was divine but said that he dared not say what Catholics thought of Mohammed out of fear of Moslem vengeance. If the Moslems would make a pact of peace and friendship with him, however, he would speak freely. The Moslems fraudulently promised faith. Perfectus then in Arabic said that Mohammed was a false prophet and a false teacher who had seduced many. In fact, he was the greatest of false prophets, filled with the trickeries of the devil, seduced by demons, given over to sacrileges, corrupting the hearts of many with venom and committing them to hell, whither he too went. How can Mohammed be a prophet and how can he avoid the curse of heaven, Perfectus asked, when he committed adultery with Zeinab, the wife of his slave Zaid? And the author of impurity had dedicated all Moslems to external impurity, Perfectus concluded. Perfectus also denounced other things in the law of Mohammed, says Eulogius, which he does not report. The Moslems were infuriated but let Perfectus go in peace then. Somewhat later, when he again passed their way, they set up a cry against him for having cursed their prophet and carried him off to the cadi.

Perfectus at first denied their charges out of fear of death, but
when he was sentenced to imprisonment and death anyway he confirmed his statements and willingly went to prison. Before he was
executed he prophesied the death within a year of the eunuch
Nasr, the prime minister . . . "who then managed the administration of the whole government in Spain." . . .

. . . . .

Perfectus died on Friday, 18 April 850, twelve days after Easter.
He was buried with pious rites by the bishop and priests in his own
church, the Basilica of St. Acisclus. Eulogius depended on the word
of Catholics who were imprisoned from the beginning with
Perfectus for his account of the martyr, he says, but Moslems too
confirmed the story. "At the time when we were in prison we found
but a few freed of all those with whom the future martyr dwelt
there," he says. These Christians had been in prison when Eulogius
met them for almost two years, from a date several months before
Perfectus' death in April 850 until November 851, when Eulogius
was imprisoned. Their fate is not known . . . The imprisonments
show that the Moslems meted out punishments other than death to
some Christians. They show too that relations between Christians
and Moslems in Córdoba were deteriorating for a year before Isaac
gave his voluntary profession of faith.

Eulogius described the Christian reaction to the death of the first
martyr and the resulting Moslem fear of the martyr movement
which they had provoked. "But such a shameful deed committed
against a priest compelled many who enjoyed a quiet and peaceful
profession of faith, contemplating God in desert mountains and
wild forests, to go forth to show their hatred for the wicked prophet
and curse him freely and publicly. And it kindled in everyone a
greater ardor of dying for justice. What the treacherous procedure
of the persecutors at first wrung by force from that one man, and
what they vengefully work against this one with persuasion and
cunning guile, afterwards raged against many who offered themselves of their own accord for such a trial. For the whole group of
pagans was shaken with exceeding terror at the step taken by the
confessors, so that they believed the ruin of the state and the downfall of their dynasty was imminent, and they pleaded suppliantly that
our athletes refrain from such pursuits." . . .

Eulogius implies that soon after the death of Perfectus Christians
came forth to curse the prophet Mohammed publicly and the

Moslems pleaded with them to stop doing so. There would have been, accordingly, voluntary public confessions of faith before that of Isaac in June 851, and Isaac's confession would have been striking only because it was delivered before the cadi, the highest official of the Moslem judicial system. Eulogius, however, regards it as Isaac's great merit that he gave his confession voluntarily. . . .

Albar in his account of the martyrdom of Perfectus makes use of his literary talent and fashions a dramatic and picturesque narrative, but he tells less about the martyr than does Eulogius. Albar indicates that Perfectus was aware of laws forbidding denunciations of Islam. As reported by Albar, Perfectus' initial denunciation of the prophet Mohammed and Islam was concerned with fleshly indulgence only and condemned Moslem marriages as adulterous. Once imprisoned, however, Perfectus made "other stronger charges." "They brought him forth," Albar says, "on that horrible paschal day of theirs, on which they are wont to eat grazing animals and to minister abundant food to their belly and their lust, and they slew him with their avenging sword."

Albar then discusses the persecution of the merchant John, whom Eulogius treats rather briefly.

"Let us go on then to treat the case of the second one. One year later, or somewhat longer, the livid eye of the Gentiles did not rest; but, as it is their wont to mock Christianity and insult all us Christians, the sellers of merchandise tried to tell lies against and to vex this John whom the walls of prison have held a long time; and burning with envy because of their love of goods they brought many charges reprehending him saying, 'Thinking little of our prophet, you always use his name in derision and to ears that do not know that you are a Christian you often confirm your lies with oaths of our religion, false as they seem to you.' Since, in good faith and not suspecting anything of the trap set for him, he wanted to show himself guiltless of those things which were charged against him, with crackling fury and blind anger he emphatically repeated the same things which he had often said, pounding them in, and saying them over and over. Then, not bearing any longer the threats of such a group, becoming angry, and adopting a rather smooth urbanity, he answered with pride and disdain, 'May the curse of God fall upon anyone who wants to call upon the name of your prophet.' At once a great clamor arose, and the close mob of damned ones, the throng full of hateful iniquity, like bees collected in one

treacherous swarm, in one heaped up mass, covered over with
malice, they led him half dead to the cadi, and when witnesses of
questionable suitability had been presented from among that crowd
of infidels, they made stronger and graver charges against him from
his own testimony. All this he denied, and he recounted the con-
suming envy which they showed in their speed against him. But the
iniquitous cadi beat him with four hundred blows of the scourge
and he made him go through the churches of all the saints while a
herald's voice cried out, 'So must he suffer who insults God's
prophet.' And then he committed him to prison under strict guard,
threatening to inflict worse things on him."

. . . . .

A few months after John's ordeal the monk Isaac came before
the cadi and voluntarily confessed what the Moslems by trickery
had succeeded in getting Perfectus and John to say. Isaac was born
of noble and wealthy citizens of Córdoba. After a privileged youth
he became an *exceptor* (secretary or official) of the state, being skilled
in Arabic. He gave up this position, however, and withdrew to the
town of Tabanos, in the wilds seven miles from Córdoba. Here a
cousin on his father's side, Jeremias, along with his wife, Elizabeth,
their family, and kin, had established a double monastery (for both
sexes), so that they might live without interruption under the law of
God. For three years Isaac lived in Tabanos under the Abbot Martin,
Elizabeth's brother, before he went down to Córdoba and voluntarily gave a confession before the cadi. . . .

Eulogius describes Isaac's confession in the preface to Book I of
the *Memoriale*. Isaac presented himself before the cadi in the forum
with these words.

" 'I would like, O cadi, to become an ardent follower of your faith
if you will at once explain to me its system and reasonableness.'
Gladly then, as if to a young tyro of his faith ready to believe . . . his
lying tongue gave forth to him the words of instruction. First he said
that Mohammed was the author of this sect, and that, enlightened
through the teaching of the angel Gabriel, he received the voice of
prophecy from the Most High to pass on to the Gentiles, founded
the law, discoursed on paradise, and taught a kingdom of heaven
full of banquets and throngs of women. And too long to be set forth
here, many other things from a religion made to conform to an
empty belief. Suddenly the youthful and venerable monk, who had

been well instructed in Arabic letters, answered him in Arabic: 'He
lied to you,' he says, '(and may he waste away under the divine
curse) who, entangled in such sin, seizes upon whole troops of lost
souls and enslaves them with himself in the depths of hell. Filled
with the devil and relying on diabolical tricks, offering the cup of
death to the sick, he shall be destroyed by eternal damnation. Why
do you who are endowed with learning not renounce such dangers?
And why do you not denounce the ulcerous and pestiferous tenets
and choose the perennial and salutary Gospel of the Christian
faith?'

These and words similar spoken by Blessed Isaac modestly but
sharply . . . cause the excited cadi quite struck out of his senses and
as if driven crazy, to burst out in abundant tears, and, seized by a
sort of mental stupidity he can hardly come to answer the monk's
reproaches. And so, reaching out he struck the face of the monk,
who said quickly, 'Do you dare to strike the visage made like the
image of God? See what account you will have to render for this.'
He was checked by the wise men sitting with him and censured
because he forgot his dignity as cadi and lightly took it on himself
to strike the martyr: especially because, according to a teaching of
their law, anyone worthy of death for a crime must not suffer the
insults of anyone at all. Then the cadi turned and spoke to Blessed
Isaac, 'Perhaps you are drunk with wine or seized with madness and
you cannot easily heed what you say. For the mind of him our
prophet, whom you rashly attack with insults, remains inexorable
and we must punish those who do not fear to say such things about
him.' The venerable Isaac stoutly made answer to him, 'Indeed, O
cadi, I am not drunk with wine nor afflicted with any sickness, but,
burning with the zeal of justice, with which your prophet and yourselves I am sure are unfamiliar, I have shown you the truth; if for
this raging death is to be the result, willingly shall I accept it,
calmly undergo it, and not move my head from its stroke. For I
know that the Lord has said, "Blessed are those who suffer persecution for justice' sake; for theirs is the kingdom of heaven"
(Mt. 5:10).' After the cadi delivered him to prison, straightway his
case became known to the king, who was exceedingly frightened
that such a charge should be made, and then and there fiercely
issues an edict to souls more fierce, saying that anyone bringing such
insults against the author of their faith shall become liable in every
instance to death. So the servant of God, condemned, submits to
death; thus is he raised up on a stake head down and placed across

the river in sight of the city, it being Wednesday, 3 June 851. After a few days his body together with those of the others who were put to death for imitating him was cremated, reduced to ashes, and then thrown into the river."

3 TRANSLATED BY *Albert S. Cook*

IBN FADLĀN'S ACCOUNT OF SCANDINAVIAN MERCHANTS ON THE VOLGA IN 922

This description of Scandinavian traders on the lower Volga is not only an interesting account of the very primitive customs of this northern people, it also shows an active trade being carried on with the Moslem world by means of Russian rivers. Most important, it gives us an idea of the superior attitude of the Moslems toward what they considered to be the dirty and lewd customs of this group of still pagan Western Europeans—an attitude that was to persist in the years to come.

I saw how the Northmen had arrived with their wares, and pitched their camp beside the Volga. Never did I see people so gigantic; they are tall as palm trees, and florid and ruddy of complexion. They wear neither camisoles nor *chaftans*, but the men among them wear a garment of rough cloth, which is thrown over one side, so that one hand remains free. Every one carries an axe, a dagger, and a sword, and without these weapons they are never seen. Their swords are broad, with wavy lines, and of Frankish make. From the tip of the finger-nails to the neck, each man of them is tattooed with pictures of trees, living beings, and other things. The women carry, fastened to their breast, a little case of iron, copper, silver, or gold, according to the wealth and resources of their husbands. Fastened to the case they wear a ring, and upon that a dagger, all attached to their breast. About their necks they wear gold and silver chains. If the husband possesses ten thousand dirhems, he has one chain made for his wife; if twenty thousand,

SOURCE. "Ibn Fadlān's Account of Scandinavian Merchants on the Volga in 922." Trans. by Albert Stanburrough Cook in *The Journal of English and Germanic Philology*, XXXIII (1923), pp. 56–63. Reprinted by permission of the University of Illinois Press.

two; and for every ten thousand, one is added. Hence it often happens that a Scandinavian woman has a large number of chains about her neck. Their most highly prized ornaments consist of small green shells, of one of the varieties which are found in [the bottoms of] ships. They make great efforts to obtain these, paying as much as a dirhem for such a shell, and stringing them as a necklace for their wives.

They are the filthiest race that God ever created. They do not wipe themselves after going to stool, nor wash themselves after a nocturnal pollution, any more than if they were wild asses.

They come from their own country, anchor their ships in the Volga, which is a great river, and build large wooden houses on its banks. In every such house there live ten or twenty, more or fewer. Each man has a couch, where he sits with the beautiful girls he has for sale. Here he is as likely as not to enjoy one of them while a friend looks on. At times several of them will be thus engaged at the same moment, each in full view of the others. Now and again a merchant will resort to a house to purchase a girl, and find her master thus embracing her, and not giving over until he has fully had his will.

Every morning a girl comes and brings a tub of water, and places it before her master. In this he proceeds to wash his face and hands, and then his hair, combing it out over the vessel. Thereupon he blows his nose, and spits into the tub, leaving no dirt behind, conveys it all into this water. When he has finished, the girl carries the tub to the man next him, who does the same. Thus she continues carrying the tub from one to another, till each of those who are in the house has blown his nose and spit into the tub, and washed his face and hair.

As soon as their ships have reached the anchorage, every one goes ashore, having at hand bread, meat, onions, milk, and strong drink, and betakes himself to a high, upright piece of wood, bearing the likeness of a human face; this is surrounded by smaller statues, and behind these there are still other tall pieces of wood driven into the ground. He advances to the large wooden figure, prostrates himself before it, and thus addresses it: "O my lord, I am come from a far country, bringing with me so and so many girls, and so and so many pelts of sable" [or, marten]; and when he has thus enumerated all his merchandise, he continues, "I have brought thee this present," laying before the wooden statue what he has brought, and saying: "I desire thee to bestow upon me a purchaser who has gold and silver coins, who will buy from me to my heart's content, and who will refuse none of my demands." Having so said, he departs. If this trade then goes ill, he returns and brings a second, or even a third present. If he still continues to have difficulty in obtaining what he desires, he brings a present to one of the small statues, and implores its intercession, saying: "These are the wives and daughters of our lord." Continuing thus, he goes to each statue in turn, invokes it, beseeches its intercession, and bows humbly before it. If it then chances that his trade goes swimmingly, and he disposes of all his merchandise, he reports: "My lord has fulfilled my desire; now it is my duty to repay him." Upon this, he takes a number of cattle and sheep, slaughters them, gives a portion of the meat to the poor, and carries the rest before the large statue and the smaller ones that surround it, hanging the heads of the sheep and cattle on the large piece of wood which is planted in the earth. When night falls, dogs come and devour it all. Then he who has so placed it exclaims: "I am well pleasing to my lord; he has consumed my present."

If one of their number falls sick, they set up a tent at a distance, in which they place him, leaving bread and water at hand. Thereafter they never approach nor speak to him, nor visit him the whole time, especially if he is a poor person or a slave. If he recovers and rises from his sick bed, he returns to his own. If he dies, they cremate him; but if he is a slave they leave as he is, till at length he becomes food of dogs and birds of prey.

If they catch a thief or a robber, they lead him to a thick and lofty tree, fasten a strong rope round him, string him up, and let him hang until he drops to pieces by the action of wind and rain.

I was told that the least of what they do for their chiefs when they die, is to consume them with fire. When I was finally informed of the death of one of their magnates, I sought to witness what befell. First they laid him in his grave—over which a roof was erected—for the space of ten days, until they had completed cutting and sewing of his clothes. In the case of a poor man, however, they merely build for him a boat, in which they place him, and consume it with fire. At the death of a rich man, they bring together his goods, and divide them into three parts. The first of these is for his family; the second is expended for the garments they make; and with the third they purchase strong drink, against the day when the girl resigns herself to death, and is burned with her master. To the use of wine they abandon themselves in mad fashion, drinking it day and night; and not seldom does one die with the cup in his hand.

When one of their chiefs dies, his family asks his girls and pages: "Which one of you will die with him?" Then one of them answers, "I." . . . For the most part . . . it is the girls that offer themselves. So, when the man of whom I spoke had died, they asked his girls, "Who will die with him?" One of them answered, "I." She was then committed to two girls, who were to keep watch over her, accompany her wherever she went, and even, on occasion, wash her feet. The people now began to occupy themselves with the dead man—to cut out the clothes for him, and to prepare whatever else was needful. During the whole of this period, the girl gave herself over to drinking and singing, and was cheerful and gay.

When the day was now come that the dead man and the girl were to be committed to the flames, I went to the river in which his ship lay, but found that it had already been drawn ashore. Four corner-blocks of birch and other woods had been placed in position for it, while around were stationed large wooden figures in the semblance of human beings. Thereupon the ship was brought up, and placed on the timbers above mentioned. In the mean time the people began to walk to and fro, uttering words which I did not understand. The dead man, meanwhile, lay at a distance in his grave, from which they had not yet removed him. Next they brought a couch, placed it in the ship, and covered it with Greek cloth of gold, wadded and quilted, with pillows of the same material. There came an old crone, whom they call the angel of death, and spread the articles mentioned on the couch. It was she who attended to the sewing of the garments, and to all the equipment; it was she, also, who was to slay the girl. I saw her; she was dark(?), . . . thick-set, with a lowering countenance.

When they came to the grave, they removed the earth from the wooden roof, set the latter aside, and drew out the dead man in the loose wrapper in which he had died. Then I saw that he had turned quite black, by reason of the coldness of that country. Near him in the grave they had placed strong drink, fruits, and a lute; and these they now took out. Except for his color, the dead man had not changed. They now clothed him in drawers, leggings, boots, and a *kurtak* and *chaftan* of cloth of gold, with golden buttons, placing on his head a cap made of cloth of gold, trimmed with sable. Then they carried him into a tent placed in the ship, seated him on the wadded and quilted covering, supported him with the pillows, and, bringing strong drinks, fruits, and basil, placed them all beside him. Then they brought a dog, which they cut in two, and threw into the ship; laid all his weapons beside him; and led up two horses, which they chased until they were dripping with sweat, whereupon they cut them in pieces with their swords, and threw the flesh into the ship. Two oxen were then brought forward, cut in pieces, and flung into the ship. Finally they brought a cock and a hen, killed them, and threw them in also.

The girl who had devoted herself to death meanwhile walked to and fro, entering one after another of the tents which they had there. The occupant of each tent lay with her, saying, "Tell your master, 'I [the man] did this only for love of you.' "

When it was now Friday afternoon, they led the girl to an object which they had constructed, and which looked like the framework of a door. She then placed her feet on the extended hands of the men, was raised up above the framework, and uttered something in her language, whereupon they let her down. Then again they raised her, and she did as at first. Once more they let her down, and then lifted her a third time, while she did as at the previous times. They then handed her a hen, whose head she cut off and threw away; but the hen itself they cast into the ship. I inquired of the interpreter what it was that she had done. He replied: "The first time she said, 'Lo, I see here my father and mother'; the second time, 'Lo, now I see all my deceased relatives sitting'; the third time, 'Lo, there is my master, who is sitting in Paradise. Paradise is so beautiful, so green. With him are his men and boys. He calls me, so bring me to him.' " Then they led her away to the ship.

Here she took off her two bracelets, and gave them to the old woman who was called the angel of death, and who was to murder her. She also drew off her two anklets, and passed them to the two serving-maids, who were the daughters of the so-called angel of death. Then they lifted her into the ship, but did not yet admit her to the tent. Now men came up with shields and staves, and handed her a cup of strong drink. This she took, sang over it, and emptied it. "With this," so the interpreter told me, "she is taking leave of those who are dear to her." Then another cup was handed her, which she also took, and began a lengthy song. The crone admonished her to drain the cup without lingering, and to enter the tent where her master lay. By this time, as it seemed to me, the girl had become dazed [or, possibly, crazed]; she made as though she would enter the tent, and had brought her head forward between the tent and the ship, when the hag seized her by the head, and dragged her in. At this moment the men began to beat upon their shields with the staves, in order to drown the noise of her out-cries, which might have terrified the other girls, and deterred them from seeking death with their masters in the future. Then six men followed into the tent, and each and every one had carnal com-panionship with her. Then they laid her down by her master's side, while two of the men seized her by the feet, and two by the hands. The old woman known as the angel of death now knotted a rope around her neck, and handed the ends to two of the men to pull. Then with a broad-bladed dagger she smote her between the ribs, and drew the blade forth, while the two men strangled her with the rope till she died.

The next of kin to the dead man now drew near, and, taking a piece of wood, lighted it, and walked backwards toward the ship, holding the stick in one hand, with the other placed upon his buttocks (he being naked), until the wood which had been piled under the ship was ignited. Then the others came up with staves and firewood, each one carrying a stick already lighted at the upper end, and threw it all on the pyre. The pile was soon aflame, then the ship, finally the tent, the man, and the girl, and everything else in the ship. A terrible storm began to blow up, and thus intensified the flames, and gave wings to the blaze.

At my side stood one of the Northmen, and I heard him talking with the interpreter, who stood near him. I asked the interpreter what the Northman had said, and received this answer: "'You Arabs,' he said, 'must be a stupid set! You take him who is to you the most revered and beloved of men, and cast him into the ground, to be devoured by creeping things and worms. We, on the other hand, burn him in a twinkling, so that he instantly, without a moment's delay, enters into Paradise.' At this he burst into un-controllable laughter, and then continued: 'It is the love of the Master [God] that causes the wind to blow and snatch him away in an instant.'" And, in very truth, before an hour had passed, ship, wood, and girl had, with the man, turned to ashes.

Thereupon they heaped over the place where the ship had stood something like a rounded hill, and, erecting on the centre of it a large birchen post, wrote on it the name of the deceased, along with that of the king of the Northmen. Having done this, they left the spot.

It is the custom among the Northmen that with the king in his hall there shall be four hundred of the most valiant and trustworthy of his companions, who stand ready to die with him or to offer their life for his. Each of them has a girl to wait upon him—to wash his head, and to prepare food and drink; and, besides her, he has another who serves as his concubine. These four hundred sit below the king's high seat, which is large, and adorned with precious stones. Accompanying him on his high seat are forty girls, destined for his bed, whom he causes to sit near him. Now and again he will proceed to enjoy one of them in the presence of the above mentioned nobles of his following. The king does not descend from his high seat, and is therefore obliged, when he needs to relieve himself, to make use of a vessel. If he wishes to ride, his horse is led up to the high seat, and he mounts from there; when he is ready to alight, he rides his horse up so close that he can step immediately from it to his throne. He has a lieutenant, who leads his armies, wars with his enemies, and represents him to his subjects.

4 FROM *Archibald R. Lewis*

THE MOSLEM EXPANSION IN THE MEDITERRANEAN, A.D. 827–960

Moslem control of the Mediterranean, which had important repercussions on Western Europe, did not begin in the seventh or eighth century, as many historians aver and Pirenne clearly stated, but during the late ninth and early tenth centuries. The way in which this happened is revealed in the following pages. However, the careful reader should note that Byzantium's naval power was never completely destroyed and that there was no overall Moslem system of naval control of the middle sea during this period. Instead, it was a fragmented Islamic political world that faced Western Europe throughout these centuries.

It might be well at this point to sum up the results of the naval action during this century and a quarter in the Mediterranean. From their positions along the coast from Syria to France the Moslems advanced into the center of the Middle Sea, beginning in 827. They established firm hold on Crete and parts of Sicily and from these centers set up advanced bases at Bari and Garigliano. In the West, a

SOURCE. Archibald R. Lewis, *Naval Power and Trade in the Mediterranean, A.D. 500–1100* (New Jersey: Princeton University Press, 1951), pp. 152–163. Reprinted by permission of the publisher and the author.

somewhat similar process was followed, though at a later date, with the Balearics playing the part of Crete and Sicily and Fraxinetum that of Bari and Garigliano. Sardinia and Cyprus were not so much occupied as neutralized by these events and played little part, except for brief periods, in this advance. The same can be said of Corsica, about which there is almost no information for this period.

The Carolingian state, which alone was affected by the Spanish Islamic advance, could not resist in any fashion. Its naval power had always been slight, and, as Charlemagne's Empire disintegrated at the end of the reign of Louis the Pious, even that slight maritime strength disappeared. Byzantium, better placed geographically, richer and better organized, resisted with more success. Its period of lowest ebb was probably about 860 when, after a great naval disaster off Sicily, Russians attacked Constantinople, Norse pirates the Hellespont, Syrians the coast of Asia Minor, and Cretans plundered widely in the Aegean.

Under Basil I, perhaps owing to a reorganization of the fleet at the time of Michael III, Constantinople enjoyed a period of resurgence on the sea. Cretans were beaten in the Aegean, and Cyprus was strongly reoccupied. With the help of Venice, Apulia was cleared of the Moslem invaders, and Nicephorus Phocas with a revived Byzantine Western fleet reestablished a firm rule over portions of Southern Italy.

This counter-offensive was stopped, however, by a great defeat off Milazzo in 888. Another period of naval decadence followed, reaching its nadir in the late years of Leo the Wise, when Taormina was lost, Salonika sacked, the Aegean in the hands of Leo of Tripoli, and perhaps there was even another assault on Constantinople by the Varangian Russians. Only the destruction of the pirate nest of Garigliano in 916, thanks largely to Fatimid internal troubles, redeemed this period from a Byzantine standpoint.

Finally, beginning at the time of Romanus Lecapenus, a thorough naval revival of Byzantium began to affect its power on the sea. Byzantine warships appeared in Western waters again in effective strength. The Aegean was clear of Leo of Tripoli's pirate fleet, and Crete was assaulted in force in 949. The Russians were badly beaten in an attack they launched on the capital in 941. And raids on Egypt in 928 and 954 reasserted naval power in that quarter for the first time in many years. The fleet of Constantinople again became a major offensive force to be reckoned with.

While Byzantium was thus revived, the Ommayids of Spain

became an important maritime power for the first time under the rule of Abd-ar-Rahman III. They not only controlled the Balearics and advance bases along the coasts of Southern France, but their naval power had to be considered by the Fatimids of Africa and Sicily as well.

The problem of just how this Moslem naval power was organized in the three major regions of its strength—Spain; North Africa and Sicily; or Crete, Syria and Egypt; remains a very difficult one to answer. Information is scanty, scattered and often confused. But at least the major outlines are apparent. In the first place, the Islamic border fleets, such as those under the Emirs of Saragossa, Tarsus, Crete and, in the early days, Palermo, seem to have been somewhat informal semi-pirate fleets manned very largely by Moslem adventurers or even Christian renegades whose primary interest was booty and plunder. Ibn Hawkal, in the late tenth century, has left a rather unflattering picture of these freebooters in his description of the quarter they inhabited at Palermo. Maqrizi, similarly describing the reorganization of the Egyptian fleet after the Byzantine raid of 853, has painted a picture of ill-paid sailors who were recruited irregularly, and were looked down on by the more respectable members of the Islamic community. Probably the organization of such border maritime forces was not much more formal than that of the land forces, who for centuries went on razzias into Christian territory along the Ebro frontier of Spain or the Taurus frontier of Byzantium. As late as the nineteenth century the pirate fleets of the Barbary coast followed a very similar pattern of organization.

This corsair character was even more pronounced in the role of such centers as Bari, Monte Garigliano and Fraxinetum. Each of these pirate nests was essentially autonomous, though Bari appears to have depended on Crete and perhaps Africa to some extent, Monte Garigliano on Sicily and Fraxinetum on Spain for support. These latter have much more in common with the buccaneers of the Caribbean in the seventeenth century than with fully organized maritime powers. The Soudan of Bari or even the Emir of Crete or Leo of Tripoli operated on the sea in a way that Henry Morgan of Port Royal eight centuries later would have thoroughly understood. The relationship of these pirates to the good Moslem merchants of Palermo, Alexandria, Tripoli, or Saragossa, or even to the Christian merchants of Naples, was not unlike that of Drake and Hawkins to those of Plymouth and Bristol, or Blackbeard to those of the

Carolina ports of North America. In Fatimid times in North Africa
there was even a government tax of one-tenth on the proceeds of
buccaneering expeditions, reminding one of Queen Elizabeth's
system in sixteenth-century England. Raiding on the sea was a
definite business and a prosperous one for the fortunate or the
skillful.

But behind this screen of advance pirate fleets and bases, the
Islamic Mediterranean world had a better naval organization of a
more fixed and regular character. This seems to have been especially true of Aghlabid and Fatimid North Africa from the ninth
century on, and of Sicily at least in the next century. There fleets
were constructed in regular arsenals, armed and manned by the
government, commanded by a series of professional sailors from
admirals down to captains, and were fully capable of taking on the
Imperial Byzantine fleet in pitched naval battles. The victories
gained by Sicilian and North African flotillas off Sicily in 859 and
888, dooming Byzantine hopes of holding this island, were by
organized naval forces.

Concerning Spain's naval organization in the tenth century, there
is a good deal of information, which probably can be applied to
other Islamic areas as well. The admiral in charge of the Spanish
Ommayid fleet was one of the four great officials of the Caliphate,
and it was said he "divided in a certain fashion royal power with
the Caliph. One reigned on the land, and the other on the sea."
Almeria was the chief naval base, and there were located the most
important naval arsenals from which the 200 ships that made up
the regular navy were equipped. There were others apparently at
Pechina, Algeciras, Silves, Alcacer do Sol, Alicante, Iviza, and
Castella de Ampurias (Tortosa). Normally some ships were stationed
at each of these bases, and in time of war would assemble at a
certain fixed rendezvous, though most probably were to be found
at Almeria and Pechina. Each ship had a captain or *caid* in charge
of the fighting men and armament and a sailing master or *rais* who
directed the sails and oars. A high official or Emir was in charge of
each major naval expedition, unless the Lord High Admiral himself
took charge. That the Fatimids had a similar organization can be
seen from their expedition against Egypt in 920 when an admiral
was in charge and contingents from Tunisia, Tripoli, and Sicily were
represented. Concerning the Eastern fleets of Syria and Egypt,
weaker in this period, there is less information except that the Emir
of Tyre seems to have been the naval commander of the Syrian

flotillas. The rendezvous point of joint Syrian-Egyptian expeditions against Byzantine territory was Cyprus, and 'the cost of a single expedition came to 100,000 dinars. There was, then, a similar careful organization of eastern Moslem as well as African and Spanish Islamic flotillas.

Another interesting point about the Moslem naval forces of the period is that they were armed either with Greek fire or a naphtha compound very much like it. The *harraquas* used by the Aghlabids off Sicily in 835 were fire ships that threw a combustible substance at enemy vessels. Leo of Tripoli used flame-throwing weapons in his attack on Salonika in 904. The Fatimid fleet which raided in the Tyrrhenian Sea in 935 *burnt* the ships it attacked. The Greek fire which was Byzantium's monopoly ceased, then, to be a terrible secret weapon as it had been in the preceding period. This may well help account for the lack of success enjoyed by Constantinople's maritime forces in much of this period. Without an advantage in their use of Greek fire, the Byzantines found control of the seas impossible to maintain. In armament, as in organization, they were little, if any, in advance of their Islamic adversaries. . . .

. . . . .

What of the effects of the changed naval situation in this period? The vital change was the passing of the important islands of the Mediterranean into Islamic hands. Control of the Crete in the East, Sicily, Malta, and Pantelleria in the center, and the Balearics in the West, with a neutralization of Sardinia and Cyprus for most of this period, had important repercussions on naval power in the Mediterranean. Practically all the major international trade routes in this sea fell into Moslem hands. Only one route was clear of threat from Islamic land and island bases. That was the route leading from the Mediterranean up the Ionian and Adriatic Seas to Venice. For thirty years even that was stopped by the Moslem bases of Bari and Tarentum. But after 875 these naval centers were captured and the Adriatic cleared. Everywhere else the narrow seas of the Mediterranean were blocked by Islamic island and advance bases—the Aegean by Crete, the Tyrrhenian by Sicily and Monte Garigliano, the Gulf of Lyons by the Balearics and Fraxinetum. Byzantium preserved, it is true, until 902 and to some extent afterwards, a hold on the straits of Messina and thus a passage from Eastern to Western Mediterranean. But its grip on these straits was uncertain, as the cooperation of Naples, Gaeta, and Amalfi with Moslem powers over and over again. In general it seems fair to say that by 878 Islam had reversed the position it held vis-à-vis Byzantium in the period from 747 to 827. Now Islamic peoples were the masters of the Middle Sea and its international trade routes.

This, of course, is to view this process from the standpoint of its effects on the northern shores of the Mediterranean; Islam bottling up the Byzantine and Western Christian peoples in the narrow seas she did not control. But there is another aspect which should be considered. Moslem control of important island positions had a defensive object or at least result. Tarsus and neutralized Cyprus were a defense of the Syrian coast; Crete protected Egypt; Sicily, North Africa, and the Balearics protected Spain. In the late ninth century, for the first time since 645, these Moslem coasts were safe from hostile assault.

They could also feel they were relatively self-sufficient in the important materials needed for naval construction. Sicily had ample stores of ship timber and some iron. North Africa, from Tunis west, had abundant timber and excellent iron deposits, and these were exploited in this period. Spain, near Tortosa, had available stands of cedar and elsewhere much oak and abundant iron. Cilicia's mountains furnished excellent wood for naval construction and Alexandretta was at this time an important port shipping timber to Egypt. Perhaps Crete was not so severely deforested at this time as it became later, but even if it were, abundant supplies of cedar and cypress were available on the Anatolian coast nearby. True, the coast from Damietta to Sousse was treeless and produced no iron. But this lack could be made up not only by shipments from Syria and the Islamic West, but also by trade in these commodities from Adriatic Venice, which possessed ample ship timber and nearby iron from Northern Italy and the Tyrol. Islamic shipping in the Mediterranean, as distinguished from such shipping in the Indian Ocean, did not suffer at this time from lack of materials.

At this point it might be well to consider the economic effects of this new Moslem control of the Mediterranean, and how it compared with that of Byzantium in the previous century. In the first place, it must be recognized that the term Islamic control is only a vague generality. There could not be any system of common overall control, except in a most general sense, because there was in this period no common political and naval unit in the Moslem lands that bordered the Middle Sea. The Dar-al-Islam was a valid con-

cept, but not in the sense of an Empire comparable to that of
Augustus, Justinian, or even Leo the Isaurian.

There were, as a matter of fact, three rather distinct naval centers
of Islamic power in the Mediterranean throughout this period: one
in the West, one in the Center, and one in the East. Of the three
probably the most important was the central nexus of Sicily and
North Africa under the Aghlabids until 909 and then controlled by
their Fatimid successors. Perhaps the all but independent and short-
lived Bari and Garigliano pirate nests should be considered as part
of this Central Moslem naval power. West of the center was the
Ommayid Spanish naval system, consisting in the ninth century of a
border fleet under the Emir of Saragossa and Fraxinetum. In the
tenth century this system broadened to include a well-organized
Spanish fleet and control over the Balearic islands. The Eastern
maritime system was the most amorphous, consisting of an independent Crete and all but autonomous Tarsus, Syrian, and Egyptian
fleets. Twice, under the late Tulunids and under the Ikshids, these
three flotillas were combined, and Crete appears always to have had
close connections with Egypt. But not infrequently, as in 904 and
935, these maritime flotillas were not united but hostile to one
another.

In general, though, there was little naval friction until the time
of the Fatimids in the early tenth century. Then territorial ambitions
caused the Fatimids to use their power on the sea against both
Eastern and Western Islamic rivals. They attacked Egypt in 914, 920,
and 935, and North African kinglets and Ommayid Spain in the
950's. Twice, in 913–917 and 937–940, their own Sicilian province
revolted as well. That there were three Caliphates (Cordova,
Medhia, and Bagdad) in this period is a proof of the disruptive
forces at work in Islam. Therefore Islamic domination of the
Mediterranean in this period was not anything approaching the
Byzantine dominion of the Middle Sea. Though they broke Byzantine maritime supremacy, the Moslems did not set up—in fact could
not set up—anything comparable to it.

5 FROM Robert S. Lopez and Irving W. Raymond
MOSLEM TRADE IN THE MEDITERRANEAN AND THE WEST

These documents and the extensive commentaries of the authors give us an excellent idea of the general remoteness of Western Europe from the Islamic world in the ninth and tenth centuries. They show that it was mainly, though not exclusively, Jewish merchants who linked the two civilizations economically. Professor Lopez's material also reveals a quickening of the pace of economic life in the entire Western Mediterranean during the tenth century. This economic upturn especially affected Italian trading centers like Amalfi, Naples, and Venice, which were already becoming important intermediaries between East and West.

MERCHANTS AND COMMERCE IN MUSLIM SYRIA

The Thousand and One Nights and other literary masterpieces have made the wealth and thriftiness of the medieval Muslin merchant familiar even to the small child. The economic history of the Muslim world, however, has been neglected by modern Arabists, and non-Arabists do not have ready access to the larger part of the sources. Hence we know little more of the commercial life of western Muslim regions during the eighth and ninth centuries than we do of the trade of the Byzantine Empire. Nor are the sources for this period really better than they are for the rest of Europe. Almost no commercial documents have been preserved. The few surviving historical, geographic, and legal works written earlier than the tenth century are often unreliable or uninteresting descriptions of trade. Usually they were written by eastern Muslims who had only indirect knowledge of the "Western Sea," as they called the Mediterranean.

One notable exception would be *The Beauties of Commerce*, by Abu al-Fadl Ja'far ibn 'Ali of Damascus, if it could be established that this was written before the tenth century. To place this work we have only a *terminus post quem* (the latest writers quoted in it are al-Jahiz— d. 864 or 869—and al-Kindi, who flourished at about the same

SOURCE. Robert S. Lopez and Irving W. Raymond, eds. and trans., *Medieval Trade in the Mediterranean World, Illustrative Documents* (New York: Columbia University Press, 1955), pp. 23–33. Reprinted by permission of the publisher.

time) and a *terminus ante quem* (a manuscript of the work copied in 1174). Hans Ritter, who made a study and a partial translation of the book, tentatively suggests the eleventh or early twelfth century because in his opinion the Muslim world before that period had not reached the commercial development indicated in the book. We believe that nothing in *The Beauties of Commerce* is incompatible with other sources on Muslim trade in the late ninth century, and we think that the lack of any mention of authorities later than that period is a decisive element of judgment.

The selection that follows (Document 1) is taken from the first part of the book, containing general considerations of business ethics and practice. We have omitted some of the leisurely sentences with which Abu al-Fadl embroiders his account. The book also has a very valuable catalogue which describes different wares.

1

[Damascus(?), Late Ninth Century(?)][1]

There are three kinds of merchants: he who travels, he who stocks, he who exports. Their trade is carried out in three ways: cash sale with a time limit for delivery, purchase on credit with payment by installments, and *muqarada*. But the *mutadammin* is not regarded as a merchant because he is nothing but a hired man of the proprietor, and the earnings upon which he relies are the payment for services rendered by him in the management and in the collection of rents. The difference between him and the managing party of a *muqarada* is the following: the managing party is not bound to indemnify [the investor] for accidental loss of the investment so long as he does not go beyond the localities agreed upon. . . .

A combination of craft and commerce occurs, for instance, in the textile and spice trades because both trades consist of two kinds of activity. They belong to the crafts because the cloth merchant must know the standards of the wares, the good and bad qualities, and fraudulent practices which go with them. Likewise, the spice merchant must know the different drugs, remedies, potions, and perfumes, their good and bad sorts as well as the counterfeits. He must know what commodities are subject to rapid change and spoil and which ones are not, and what means ought to be used to

---

[1] From Abu al-Fadl Ja'far ibn 'Ali al-Dimishqui, *The Beauties of Commerce*.

preserve and to restore them, and lastly he also must understand the blends of electuaries and potions, of powders and drugs. The textile merchant must also understand the folding and display of the wares and what means are used to store them. But both the spice merchants and the cloth merchants belong to the class of merchants because they buy and sell and draw their profit therefrom, and so forth. . . .

Know, my brother—may God guide you to what is dear and agreeable to Him—that the rule of the operations of the merchant who stocks consists in buying the wares in the time of their season and whenever the importation is uninterrupted, the supply large, and the demand small. . . .

This type of merchant above all needs early information on the relative situation of wares in their places of origin and native lands, whether the quantity on hand is great or small, cheap or dear, whether business has prospered abundantly and is in a good state or whether it has turned out poorly and has deteriorated, whether the import routes are cut off or are safe. He must try to obtain the knowledge of all this through inquiries and precise questioning of the caravans. . . .

When the merchant who stocks has made up his mind and is resolved to buy a ware, for instance, at 200 dinars cash, he ought not to buy all at once but to divide the purchase into four different times separated by intervals of fifteen days, so that the entire purchase is concluded within two months, the reason being that the price of the purchased ware either ceaselessly rises and falls or else remains steady. Now if after the purchase of one part the price goes up, he knows that this promises him profit and makes gain possible; and he should be happy about it, if indeed he is a moderate man and values a profit made through foresighted consideration more highly than a dangerous speculation. If, however, the ware becomes cheaper, he can then be happy in two respect, first, because he has remained protected against the fall in price which would have hit him if he had purchased the whole and, second, because he now has the opportunity to buy good wares cheaply. Should, however, the price remain unchanged at the same level, his eye is sharpened to seize the right moment for buying and stocking wares. But if he buys everything in great haste at one time, then something that he has not considered is sure to happen to him, and now he seeks to make up the loss. From this, then, arise the controversies and lawsuits which are so frequent in this profession. . . .

The merchant who travels must, above all, pay attention to what kinds of wares he buys, and here he must exercise great caution. He also ought not to lull himself into the belief that his hopes must necessarily be fulfilled on arrival at the desired destination, because the journey may very easily be delayed or become impossible through some obstacle, perhaps because the route is dangerous or the winds unfavorable to a sea voyage, or because some unforeseen event takes place in the locality to which he wishes to travel. Such things may easily happen to a merchant. He must then sell the ware, for better or for worse, where he has bought it; and if he has not prepared himself in advance for such a contingency, he will suffer a great loss in its price. . . .

Further, it is worthy of note that he should carry with him a price list of all the wares of the locality to which he will return. . . . When he wants to buy an article, he establishes by this record the difference in price of the ware in the two places, takes into account the provisions he will need up to the time of his return, adds to the price list a list of the different tolls in the country, and calculates the profit. . . .

The merchant who arrives in a locality unknown to him must also carefully arrange in advance to secure a reliable representative, a safe lodging house, and whatever besides is necessary, so that he is not taken in by a slow payer or by a cheat. . . .

Know, my brother—may God guide you—that the operations of the merchant who exports consist in employing in the locality to which he exports some one who takes care of the wares sent to him. The latter is then entrusted with selling the wares and with buying others in exchange, and he ought to be a trustworthy, reliable, and well-to-do man who has devoted himself fully to commerce and who is also well experienced in it. The goods are shipped to him, and the entire selling is placed in his hands. He receives a share of the gain of all that he buys or sells. If a ware is low in supply, he may stock it, if he thinks it wise. The wares which are sent him must correspondingly be bought with care and shipped prior to the time of the fair in the best quality and in the best condition possible. Therefore one must endeavor to buy the wares with the possibility of extending the term of payment, with easy conditions of payment, and with rights of option. If this is not possible with one ware, one should try to obtain it with another; for the profit, with the assistance of God, depends on suitable purchase.

Lastly, one must send a ware only with reliable carriers who keep

it under their protection until it is received by the appointed representative.

THE FLOW OF MERCHANDISE TO THE HEART OF THE MUSLIM WORLD

Syria was still a thriving province when Abu al-Fadl wrote his
book, but it was no longer the heart of the Muslim world. The
capital of the Caliphate had been moved from Damascus to
Baghdad in 750. There is no lack of source material, translated
or analyzed, in English, dealing with Baghdad. Hence we present
here a passage referring not to the city alone but to the entire province, Iraq or Mesopotamia. The natural maritime outlet of this
region was the Persian Gulf, but the Mediterranean was close
enough to be accessible to caravans coming from Iraq. Muslim
writers often stress the influence and activity of Iraqi merchants in
Egypt and in other Mediterranean countries.

Document 2 lists wares coming from all parts of the world. It is
taken from *The Investigation of Commerce,* a pamphlet ascribed to a
famous writer, Amr ibn Bahr of Basra, surnamed al-Jahiz (d. 864 or
869). The attribution has been challenged, even though his name
appears in the manuscript. But certainly the picture given in the
pamphlet reflects the commercial currents of the ninth century as
we know them in other sources. Mediterranean countries appear less
important in trade than does the Asiatic East. Although 'the borders
of the Maghrib' (i.e., the westernmost part of North Africa), Barbary, and Egypt are mentioned among regions exporting wares to
Mesopotamia, the larger part comes from the eastern Muslim
world, India and China. Non-Muslim countries in the list include
Armenia and the Khazar state of the lower Volga. The former carried on much of the border trade between the Muslim states and the
Byzantine Empire. The latter was an important channel of trade of
Muslim merchants with the Slavs and other European peoples.

2

[Iraq, Mid-Ninth Century][2]

IMPORTS OF IRAQ

From India are imported tigers(?), panthers, elephants, panther
skins, rubies, white sandal, ebony, and coconuts.

[2] From Al-Jahiz(?), *The Investigation of Commerce.*

From China are imported silk stuffs, silk, chinaware, paper, ink, peacocks, racing horses, saddles, felts, cinnamon, Greek unblended rhubarb. [Also] are imported utensils of gold and silver, *qaysarani* dinars of pure gold, drugs, brocades, racing horses, female slaves, knicknacks with human figures, fast locks . . . hydraulic engineers, expert agronomists, marble workers, and eunuchs.

From Arabia: Arab horses, ostriches, pedigreed she-camels, *qan* wood, and tanned skins.

From Barbary and the borders of Maghrib: panthers, *salam* leaves, felts, and black hawks.

From Yemen: collyrium, tanned skins, giraffes, cuirasses, colored gems, incense, *khitr* leaves, and curcuma.

From Egypt: trotting donkeys, suits of fine cloth, papyrus, balsam, and—from its mines—topazes of superior quality.

From the land of the Khazars: slaves of both sexes, coats of mail, helmets, and camails of [chain] mail.

From the land of Khwarizm: musk; ermine, marten, miniver, and fox furs; and very sweet sugar cane.

From Samarkand: paper.

From Balkh and its region: sweet grapes and *ghawshana* truffles.

From Bushanj: candied capers.

From Merv: zither players, valuable zithers, carpets, and Merv suits.

From Gurgan: grapes of various sorts, pheasants, excellent pomegranate grains, cloaks of soft wool, excellent raw silk.

From Amid: brocaded suits, scarfs, fine curtains, and woolen veils for the head.

From Damawand: arrow heads.

From Rayy: prunes, mercury, woolen cloaks, weapons, fine suits, combs, "royal" bonnets, *qussiyat* linen cloth, and pomegranates.

From Ispahan: refined and raw honey, quinces, China pears, apples, salt, saffron, soda, white-lead, antimony sulphide, beds of several decks, extra fine suits, and fruit syrups.

From Qumis: axes, saddle felts, parasols, and woolen veils for the head.

From Kirman: indigo and cumin.

From Ghur: cuirasses and psyllium.

From Barda'a: fast mules.

From Nisibin: lead.

From Fars: *tawwazi* and *saburi* linen suits, rose water, water-lily ointment, jasmine ointment, and syrups.

From Fasa: pistachios, various sorts of fruit, rare fruit, and glass ware.

From Oman and the seacoast: pearls.

From Ahwaz and the surrounding region: sugar and silk brocades . . . castanets, dancing girls . . . extract of grapes, various sorts of dates, and sugar candy.

From Sus: citrons, violet ointment, basil, horsecloth, and pack-saddles.

From Mosul: curtains, striped cloth, francolins, and quail.

From Hulwan: pomegranates, figs, and vinegar sauces.

From Armenia and Azerbaijan: felts . . . packsaddles, carpets, fine mats, cordons for drawers, and wool.

THE JEWISH ROLE IN WORLD TRADE

Jewish merchants had a very large share of the meager trade of the early Middle Ages. In the more backward regions of Western Europe, such as the interior provinces of France and Germany, they seem to have held almost a monopoly of international commerce. They were less prominent in the highly developed Byzantine and Muslim territories, but even there they were second to none in the scope of their travels.

Our first selection (Document 3), taken from the geographical work of Ibn Khurradadhbah, describes Western Europe as it was hazily known to a scholar living in Persia in the ninth century. The second selection (Document 4), from the same source, outlines the itineraries of the Jewish merchants called al-Radhaniyya. It will be noted that Western European place names and articles of trade mentioned in the first selection are almost exactly the same as those mentioned in the second selection describing the scope of trade of Jewish merchants.

3

[Between 846 and 886][3]

. . . Rome, Bulgaria, the countries of the Slavs and the Avars are to the north of Spain.

[3] From Abu al-Qasim ʻUbayd Allah ibn Khurradadhbah, *The Book of the Routes and the Kingdoms.*

Through the Sea of the Maghrib, are exported Slavic, Roman, Frankish, and Lombard slaves; Roman and Spanish girls; beaver skins and other furs; among the perfumes, may'a; and among the drugs, mastic. From the bottom of the sea, close to Frankish territory, comes bussadh, a material usually known by the name of marjan.

The sea which stretches beyond the country of the Slavs and on the shore of which is the city of Tulia is not frequented by any ship or boat, and no products are exported from it. Likewise, the Western Ocean, where the Fortunate Islands are situated, has not been explored by navigators and does not supply any object for consumption.

4

[Between 846 and 886][4]

ROUTES OF THE JEWISH MERCHANTS CALLED AL-RADHANIYYA

These merchants speak Arabic, Persian, Roman, Frankish, Spanish, and Slavonic. They travel from the East to the West and from the West to the East by land as well as by sea. They bring from the West eunuchs, slave girls, boys, brocade, beaver skins, marten furs and other varieties of fur, and swords. They embark in the land of the Franks on the Western Sea, and they sail toward al-Farama. There they load their merchandise on the backs of camels and proceed by land to al-Qulzum, twenty-five parasangs distant. They embark on the Eastern Sea and proceed from al-Qulzum to al-Jar and to Jidda; then they go to Sind, Hind, and China. On their return from China they load musk, aloe wood, camphor, cinnamon, and other products of the eastern countries and they come back to al-Qulzum, then to al-Farama, and from there they embark again on the Western Sea. Some of them sail for Constantinople in order to sell their merchandise to the Romans. Others proceed to the residence of the king of the Franks to dispose of their articles.

Sometimes the Jewish merchants, embarking in the country of the Franks on the Western Sea, sail toward Antioch. From there they proceed by land to al-Jabiya, where they arrive after three days' journey. There they take a boat on the Euphrates and they reach Baghdad, from where they go down the Tigris to al-Ubullah. From

[4] From Abu al-Qasim 'Ubayd Allah ibn Khurradadhbah, *The Book of the Routes and the Kingdoms.*

al-Ubullah they sail for, successively, Oman, Sind, Hind, and China. . . .

These different journeys may likewise be made by land. Merchants leaving from Spain or France proceed to Sus al-Aqsa and then to Tangier, and from there they set out for Africa and to the capital of Egypt. From there they turn toward al-Ramla; visit Damascus, Kufa, Baghdad, and Basra; cross al-Ahwaz, Fars, Kirman, Sind, and Hind; and reach China. Sometimes also they take the route back of Rome, and, crossing the country of the Slavs, proceed to Khamlij, the capital of the Khazars. They embark on the Caspian Sea, then reach Balkh and Transoxiana, then continue the journey toward the camp of the Tughuzghur, and from there to China.

PART TWO

Contact and Disillusion—From the First Crusade to the End of the Latin Kingdom of Jerusalem, A.D. 1095–1291

During the last half of the eleventh century, a new era began in Western European–Moslem relations. Spanish Christians and their French allies advanced deep into Islamic Spain to begin the *Reconquista* (Selection 1). Norman adventurers conquered Sicily, while their Genoese and Pisan allies cleared Sardinia and Corsica of Moslems and, impelled by a Seljuk Turkish advance into Anatolia and Syria, the First Crusaders began a conquest of Palestine and Syria (Selection 2).

Because of this expansion a large number of Moslems in Spain, Sicily, and the Near East found themselves, for the first time, under Western Christian rule. And now, despite raids on Moslem Mediterranean ports, economic and cultural contacts multiplied steadily. In addition to all this, a century later, after Byzantium had fallen to the West in the Fourth Crusade and the Mongols had extended their rule into Russia and Western Asia, Italian merchants and adventurers and Christian churchmen alike became acquainted with Moslem Iraq, Persia, and India.

At first these new contacts between Western Christendom and Islam were relatively satisfactory and even fruitful and profitable for both civilizations, especially in Spain and Sicily where religious toleration proved the wisest course for rulers to adopt. But by the late twelfth century, things had begun to change. This was the result of a vigorous Moslem reaction in the Near East led by Saladin (Selection 3) and a somewhat similar militancy in Moslem Spain on the part of the fanatical North African Almohads. Out of these movements emerged a vigorous, orthodox Islamic society, but one which was considerably narrower in its religious and cultural emphases

than before. This society continued relatively unchanged into the thirteenth
century. It proved resilient enough to withstand the shock of Mongol
invasions and produce rulers in Mamluke Egypt who drove Western
European conquerors from Palestine and Syria by 1291. Very likely it is this
new Moslem mood which explains the survival of the Kingdom of Granada
in Spain.

At the very time that Moslem society was slowly moving toward an
attitude of hostility in its dealings with the West, its civilization was
having a considerable impact on Latin Christendom as a whole. Nowhere
was this truer than in the Kingdom of Two Sicilies where rulers copied
Islamic administrative practices and culture extensively, acting almost as
Christian Sultans (Selection 4). In the economic sphere also, extensive
trade contacts, maintained and expanded by Italian and Catalan merchants
throughout the Mediterranean, linked the economy of the extensive Islamic
world with that of Western Europe and resulted in an improvement of
Western business practices (Selection 5). Finally, these contacts, primarily
in Spain and Sicily, resulted in the transmission of superior Moslem philosophy and science to eager Western intellectuals, who used it to help build a
new European civilization (Selection 6).

Unfortunately, however, during these two centuries the Islamic world
saw little in Western European culture that interested it, and its hostility
toward the West deepened progressively. This was particularly so in the
later thirteenth century when the Mongol menace frightened Moslem
intellectuals and narrowed and weakened the culture which they had to
offer to their own upper classes. It was this defensive attitude that now
passed on to future Islamic generations.

1 TRANSLATED BY *Merriam Sherwood*

SELECTION FROM THE POEM OF THE CID

The Poem of the Cid, *though it dates from the mid-twelfth century in its present form, deals with a great hero, the Cid, who lived during the last years of the eleventh century and won fame and great riches fighting along the Moslem frontier of Spain. Although most of his activities were directed against Moslem enemies and he ended his life as the conqueror of the Islamic kingdom of Valencia, this selection, which tells of his battle against the Christian Count of Barcelona, shows that he was perfectly willing to fight fellow Christians if the occasion warranted. The poem thus shows a fluidity of loyalties and purpose during the period of the* Reconquista *in Spain which seems remarkable indeed.*

. . . The Cid spurred onward, and took his stand on a hill which is above Monreal. High is the hill, marvelous and big. He did not fear attack, you may know, from any side. First he placed under tribute Daroca, then Molina, which was on the other side, then Teruel, which was in front of him. He held in his hand Cella, the one called 'del Canal.'

May the Cid Ruy Díaz have the grace of God! Alvar Fáñez Minaya had gone to Castile. He presented thirty horses to the King. The King saw them and smiled a fair smile:

'Who is the giver of these? May God keep you, Minaya!'

SOURCE. *The Tale of the Warrior Lord*, trans. by Merriam Sherwood (copyright 1930 by Longmans, Green & Co.; copyright renewed 1958 by Merriam Sherwood), pp. 40–47. Reprinted by permission of David McKay Co., Inc.

41

'The Cid Ruy Díaz, who in lucky hour girded on his sword. After
he lost your grace, he won from the Moors the castle of Alcocer. The
Moors sent word to the King of Valencia, who dispatched his forces
with two Moorish kings against him. They besieged him there and
cut off the water from him, so that we could not hold out. Then the
Cid decided to sally forth against them, and we fought a pitched
battle, and the Cid had the victory. He conquered the two Moorish
kings in that battle. Exceeding great, Lord, was the booty. He sends
this present to you, honored King. He kisses your feet and both your
hands. May you have mercy on him. The Creator protect you!'
    Said the King:
    'It is very soon, after such a short time, to pardon a man in dis-
grace with his lord! But I accept this gift since it was taken from the
Moors. What is more, I am pleased with the Cid for winning such
spoils. Besides this, I acquit you, Minaya. I give you back your
fiefs and your lands. You may go and come freely. From now on you
have my pardon. But of the Cid Campeador I say nothing to you.
Yet in addition I will say to you that any men, good and valiant, in
all my kingdom, who wish to aid the Cid may do so without fear that
I will seize their bodies or their lands.'
    Minaya Alvar Fáñez kissed the King's hands, and said:
    'Thanks and thanks again, King, as to my rightful lord. You do
this now; later on you will do more.'
    Said the King:
    'Go through Castile and tell them to let you pass. Go, without
fear, to find the Cid.'
    I will tell you now of him who in lucky hour girded on his sword.
That hill on which he pitched his camp, as long as there are Moorish
and Christian people, will be written *El Poyo de Mio Cid,* 'The Hill
of the Cid.' While he was there he pillaged all around. He laid under
tribute the whole valley of the Martín River. News of him reached
Saragossa, and did not please the Moors of that city at all. The Cid
was there fifteen whole weeks. When the Chief saw that Minaya was
delayed, he made a night march with all his men. He left El Poyo,
'The Hill,' and took everything away. Don Rodrigo passed on the
other side of Teruel. Ruy Díaz camped in the pine-grove of Tévar.
He pillaged all those lands, and laid Saragossa under tribute.
    After he had done this, at the end of three weeks, Minaya came
back from Castile. He brought two hundred with him, all girt with
swords; and footsoldiers besides, you may know, without number.
When the Cid caught sight of Minaya he went—his horse running—

to embrace him. He kissed him on the mouth and on the eyes of his face. Minaya hid nothing from him but told him everything. The Campeador smiled a fair smile:

'Thanks be to God and to His holy powers! While you live, it will go well with me, Minaya!'

Dios! How joyful was all that host; for Minaya Alvar Fáñez brought them greetings from cousins and from brothers and from wives whom they had left behind. *Dios!* How joyful was he of the beautiful beard, because Alvar Fáñez had paid for the thousand Masses and had brought greetings from his wife and his daughters. *Dios!* How pleased was the Cid, and how great was his joy!

'How now, Alvar Fáñez! may you live many days!'

He who in lucky hour was born did not linger. He made the lands of Alcañiz black, and round about he pillaged everything. On the third day he returned.

The news had spread through all the country. Those of Monzón were worried and those of Huesca. Those of Saragossa were glad, because they paid tribute, and so feared no harm from the Cid Ruy Díaz.

Those of the Cid went back to the camp with the booty. They were all joyful, for the spoils were large. The Cid was pleased, and much pleased was Alvar Fáñez. The Chief smiled; he could not help his words:

'What ho! Knights, I will tell you the truth: he who bides always in one place may lose what he has. Tomorrow morning let us ride away. We shall leave this camp and go further.'

Then the Cid moved to the Pass of Olocau. From there he made a run to Huesa and to Montalbán. They spent ten days in that foray. The news went everywhere that the exile from Castile was bringing them all this evil.

The news had gone everywhere. Word came to the Count of Barcelona, Don Ramón, that the Cid Ruy Díaz was overrunning all the land. He was very angry, for he held it a great insult. The Count was a mighty boaster and he said a foolish thing:

'Deep are the wrongs done to me by the Cid of Vivar. He did me a great wrong once within my court: he struck my nephew and never made amends. Now he is overrunning the lands that are under my protection. I have not challenged him nor forsworn my friendship with him; but since he provokes me, I am going to demand satisfaction.'

His forces were large, and they gathered hastily. What with Moors and Christians, many troops joined him. They went after the Cid, the good Knight of Vivar. They marched for three days and two nights. They overtook him in the pine-grove of Tévar. With their strong forces they thought to make him prisoner.

The Cid Don Rodrigo was bringing back large booty. He was going down from a mountain top and had reached a valley. A message came to him from the Count Don Ramón. The Cid sent thither after he had heard it:

'Tell the Count not to take it ill. I have nothing of his; let him suffer me to go in peace.'

The Count answered:

'That shall not be! For that other wrong and for this one now he shall make full amends. The Exile shall know whom he has come to insult!'

The messenger went back as quickly as he could. Then the Cid of Vivar knew that they could not get off without a battle.

'What ho! Knights! place the booty to one side. Get ready quickly and put on your armor. Don Ramón the Count is going to give us a great battle. He leads large troops of Moors and of Christians. He refuses to let us go without a fight. Since they would pursue us further, let the battle be here. Get the horses ready and put on your armor. They are coming down the hill, all wearing hose, and they have light saddles with loose girths. We shall ride on Galician saddles and wear boots over our hose! We, a hundred knights, ought to vanquish those troops. Before they reach the plain let us have at them with our lances. For one whom you strike three saddles will go empty. Ramón Berenguer shall see whom he pursued today to the pine-grove of Tévar, to take his booty from him.'

They all put on their armor after the Cid had ended. They took their arms and mounted their horses. They saw the army of the Franks of Catalonia coming down. At the foot of the hill, near the plain, the Cid, he who in lucky hour was born, gave the command to strike. His men obeyed gladly. They used their bannered lances so well, smiting some and overthrowing others, that he who in lucky hour was born won that battle. He took prisoner Don Ramón the Count. The Cid won there the sword *Colada*, that was worth more than a thousand marks.

He gained that battle, with more honor to his beard. He took the Count captive and led him to his tent. He ordered his henchmen to guard him. The Cid sprang out of his tent. His men were gathering from all sides. The Cid was pleased, for the booty was large. They prepared a great feast for the Cid Don Rodrigo.

The Count Don Ramón did not care for the feast at all. They brought in the viands and placed them before him. He would not eat but scorned everything:

'For all that is in Spain I would not eat a mouthful. I would rather lose my body and my life, since men so ill-shod have vanquished me in battle!'

You shall hear what the Cid Ruy Díaz said:

'Eat some of this bread, Count, and drink some of this wine. If you will do as I say you shall go free. If not, in all your life you will not see Christendom.'

'Eat, Don Rodrigo, and enjoy yourself. I shall let myself die, for I do not want to eat.'

Until the third day they could not persuade him. They could not make him take a mouthful of bread while they were dividing that great booty. Said the Cid:

'Eat something, Count, for if you do not, you will not see Christendom. And, if you eat so that I am satisfied, I will set you free and liberate you, you and two nobles.'

When the Count heard this he began to rejoice:

'If you do as you have said, Cid, I shall wonder at it as long as I live.'

'Then eat, Count, and when you have dined, you and two others, I will set you free. But of what you have lost and I won in the field, be sure that I shall not give you one miserable farthing; for I need it for these my vassals, who follow me in poverty. I will not give that back to you. By taking from you and from others we shall be satisfied. We shall lead this life as long as it shall please the Holy Father—this life of an exile whose king is angry with him.'

The Count was joyful. He asked for water for his hands and they brought it quickly to him. With the knights whom the Cid had granted him, the Count ate—*Dios!* With what good will! Just above him at the table sat he who in lucky hour was born:

'If you do not eat well, Count, so as to satisfy me, we shall stay here, we two shall not part.'

Then the Count said:

'I shall be glad to do as you wish.'

With those two knights he dined quickly. The Cid, who was looking at them, was delighted to see how deftly Don Ramón used his hands.

'If you please, Cid, we are ready to go. Have our beasts brought and we will mount at once. From the day I became Count I have not eaten with such pleasure. It is one that I shall not forget.'

They gave them three palfreys very well saddled, and good clothing: furred tunics and mantles. The Count Don Ramón rode between the two nobles. The Castilian escorted them to the end of the camp.

'Already you are going, Count,' he said, 'as a Frank, or free man, should. I thank you for what you have left me. If it should enter your mind to seek vengeance, and if you should come after me, send me word first: either you will leave me something of yours or take something of mine.'

'Rejoice, O Cid, you are quite safe. I have paid you for all this year. I shall not even think of coming to seek you.'

The Count dug in his spurs and rode away. He kept turning his head and looking round. He was afraid that the Cid would repent—which the Cid would not have done for anything in the world; for he was a man of his word.

The Count was gone. He of Vivar returned. He joined his followers and began to distribute the booty that they had taken—marvelous and great. His men were so rich that they did not know what they had.

2 TRANSLATED BY   *H. A. R. Gibb*

EXTRACTS FROM AL-QALANISI'S DAMASCUS CHRONICLE OF THE CRUSADES

The following excerpts from this Moslem chronicle deal with the first period of crusading activities in Syria and Palestine down to 1105. These years saw four crusading principalities established on firm bases. Our excerpts reveal the hostility which existed among Moslem principalities in the region, such as Shiah Egypt and Orthodox Damascus, and the anti-Turkish attitudes of the Arabic speaking Syrian Moslems. We even see here the initial activities of the Moslem sect of the Assassins in 1105. Under the circumstances it does not seem remarkable that the Crusaders were able to establish themselves in this part of the world and that Moslem resistance was spasmodic, ill-organized, and unenthusiastic.

28th November, 1098, to 16th November, 1099

In Muharram of this year (December, 1098), the Franks made an assault on the wall of Ma'arrat al-Nu'mān from the east and north. They pushed up the tower until it rested against the wall, and as it was higher, they deprived the Muslims of the shelter of the wall. The fighting raged round this point until sunset on 14th Muharram (11th December), when the Franks scaled the wall, and the towns-folk were driven off it and took flight. Prior to this, messengers had repeatedly come to them from the Franks with proposals for a settlement by negotiation and the surrender of the city, promising in return security for their lives and property, and the establishment of a [Frankish] governor amongst them, but dissension among the citizens and the fore-ordained decree of God prevented acceptance of these terms. So they captured the city after the hour of the sunset prayer, and a great number from both sides were killed in it. The townsfolk fled to the houses of al-Ma'arra, to defend themselves in them, and the Franks, after promising them safety, dealt treacherously with them. They erected crosses over the town, exacted

SOURCE. *The Damascus Chronicle of the Crusades*, extracted and trans. from *The Chronicle of Ibn al-Qalanisi* by H. A. R. Gibb (London: Luzac & Co., Ltd., 1932), pp. 46–59. Reprinted by permission of the publisher.

indemnities from the townsfolk, and did not carry out any of the terms upon which they had agreed, but plundered everything that they found, and demanded of the people sums which they could not pay. On Thursday 17th Safar (13th January, 1099) they set out for Kafr Tāb.

Thereafter they proceeded towards Jerusalem, at the end of Rajab (middle of June) of this year, and the people fled in panic from their abodes before them. They descended first upon al-Ramla, and captured it after the ripening of the crops. Thence they marched to Jerusalem, the inhabitants of which they engaged and blockaded, and having set up the tower against the city they brought it forward to the wall. At length news reached them that al-Afdal was on his way from Egypt with a mighty army to engage in the Holy War against them, and to destroy them, and to succour and protect the city against them. They therefore attacked the city with increased vigour, and prolonged the battle that day until the daylight faded, then withdrew from it, after promising the inhabitants to renew the attack upon them on the morrow. The townsfolk descended from the wall at sunset, whereupon the Franks renewed their assault upon it, climbed up the tower, and gained a footing on the city wall. The defenders were driven down, and the Franks stormed the town and gained possession of it. A number of the townsfolk fled to the sanctuary [of David], and a great host were killed. The Jews assembled in the synagogue, and the Franks burned it over their heads. The sanctuary was surrendered to them on guarantee of safety on the 22nd of Sha 'bān (14th July) of this year, and they destroyed the shrines and the tomb of Abraham. Al-Afdal arrived with the Egyptian armies, but found himself forestalled, and having been reinforced by the troops from the Sāhil, encamped outside Ascalon on 14th Ramadān (4th August), to await the arrival of the fleet by sea and of the Arab levies. The army of the Franks advanced against him and attacked him in great force. The Egyptian army was thrown back towards Ascalon, al-Afdal himself taking refuge in the city. The swords of the Franks were given mastery over the Muslims, and death was meted out to the footmen, volunteers, and townsfolk, about ten thousand souls, and the camp was plundered. Al-Afdal set out for Egypt with his officers, and the Franks besieged Ascalon, until at length the townsmen agreed to pay them twenty thousand dinars as protection money, and to deliver this sum to them forthwith. They therefore set about collecting this amount from the inhabitants of the town, but it befel that a quarrel broke out between the [Frankish] leaders, and they retired without having received any of the money. It is said that the number of the people of Ascalon who were killed in this campaign—that is to say of the witnesses, men of substance, merchants, and youths, exclusive of the regular levies—amounted to two thousand seven hundred souls.

. . . . .

6th November, 1100, to 25th October, 1101

In this year, the amīr Sukmān b. Ortuq collected a great host of Turkmens, and marched with them against the Franks of al-Ruhā (Edessa) and Sarūj, in the month of First Rabī' (January, 1101). He captured Sarūj, and was joined by a large body [of volunteers], while the Franks also collected their forces. When the two armies met, the Muslims were on the point of victory over them, but it happened that a party of the Turkmens fled and Sukmān lost heart and retired. The Franks then advanced to Sarūj, recaptured it, and killed and enslaved its inhabitants, except those of them who escaped by flight.

In this year also, Godfrey, lord of Jerusalem, appeared before the fortified port of 'Akkā and made an assault upon it, but he was struck by an arrow and killed. Prior to this he had rebuilt Yāfā (Jaffa) and given it in charge to Tancred. When Godfrey was killed, his brother Baldwin the count, lord of al Ruhā, set out for Jerusalem with a body of five hundred knights and footmen. On hearing the report of his passage, Shams al-Mulūk Duqāq gathered his forces and moved out against him, together with the amīr Janāh al-Dawla, lord of Hims, and they met him near the port of Bairūt. Janāh al-Dawla pressed forward towards him with his 'askar, and he defeated him and killed some of his companions.

In this year the Franks captured Haifā, on the sea coast, by assault, and Arsūf by capitulation, and they drove its inhabitants out of it. At the end of Rajab also (end of May) they captured Qaisarīya by assault, with the assistance of the Genoese, killed its population, and plundered everything in it.

In Sha 'bān of this year (June, 1101), the qādī Ibn Sulaiha, who had made himself master of the fortified port of Jabala, wrote to Zahīr al-Dīn Atābek, requesting him to select and send a trustworthy officer, that he might hand over to him the fortress of Jabala, and

himself retire with all his property to Damascus, and that he would
convey him thence to Baghdād with an escort, and under guarantee
of safe conduct, protection, and honourable treatment. The Atābek
consented to this proposal, and promised to carry his desire into
effect, and deputed as governor of the port his son, the amīr Tāj al-
Mulūk Būrī. The king Shams al-Mulūk Duqāq was at the time
absent from Damascus in Diyār Bakr, and he returned thence and
entered Damascus on 1st Shawwāl (30th July). The arrangements
were confirmed according to Ibn Sulaiha's request, and Tāj al-
Mulūk set out with his train for Jabala, and took it over.

Ibn Sulaiha departed thence and arrived at Damascus with his
followers, goods and effects, baggage and riding-beasts, and all that
he possessed of money, movable property, and estate. He was
received with honour and richly entertained, and after a stay of
some days at Damascus was conveyed to Baghdād with everything
that he possessed by a strong detachment of troops. When he
arrived, it came about that some person denounced him and gave
such a report of his riches to the Sultan of Baghdād, that he was
plundered and all that he possessed fell into the Sultan's hands.

As for Tāj al-Mulūk, when he took possession of the fortress of
Jabala and he and his followers were firmly established there,
they ill-treated its people and behaved evilly towards them, and
acted contrary to the approved custom of justice and fair dealing.
The townsfolk therefore sent a complaint of their condition under
the misfortune that had befallen them to the Qādī Fakhr al-Mulk,
Abū 'Alī 'Ammār b. Muḥammad b. 'Ammār, who had seized the
fortified port of Tarābulus (Tripolis), on account of the proximity
of Tarābulus to their town. He promised to assist them to attain
their object, and to send them support, and dispatched to them a
considerable force from his 'askar, which entered the town and,
having joined with its people against the Turks, defeated and drove
them out, and took possession of it. They captured Tāj al-Mulūk
and carried him to Tarābulus where Fakhr al-Mulk received him
honourably, treated him kindly, and sent him back to Damascus,
together with a letter to his father informing him of the state of
affairs and presenting his excuses to him for what had happened.

26th October, 1101, to 14th October, 1102

In this year reports were brought to the effect that the peoples of Khurāsān, 'Irāq, and Syria were in a state of constant bickering and hatred, wars and disorder, and fear of one another, because their rulers neglected them and were distracted from the task of governing them by their dissensions and mutual warfare.

In this year also the Count of al-Ruhā, the commander of the Franks, arrived with his God-forsaken troops at the fortified port of Bairūt, and encamped over against it, in the hope of capturing it. He remained before it for a long time, attacking and besieging the town, but his ambition could not be realized, and he raised the siege and departed.

Letters arrived from Fakhr al-Mulk Ibn 'Ammār, lord of Tarābulus, beseeching aid in driving back the son of St. Gilles, who had descended with his army of Franks on Tarābulus, and asking for the assistance of the 'askar of Damascus. His request was granted, and the 'askar set off towards him. The amir Janāh al-Dawla, lord of Hims, was summoned also, and he too arrived with his 'askar. Their armies united and marched in brave force in the direction of Antartūs (Tortosa). The Franks hastened towards them with their host and levies, and the two armies approached one another and engaged in battle there. The army of the Muslims was shattered by the army of the infidels, and a great number of them were killed. Those who escaped retreated to Damascus and Hims, after suffering considerable losses, and arrived on 23rd Latter Jumādā (14th April, 1102).

In this year also the Egyptian armies came up from Egypt to assist the governors of the Sāhil in those fortified ports which still remained in their hands against the besieging parties of the Franks. They reached Ascalon in Rajab (April–May), and when Baldwin, Count of Jerusalem, learned of their arrival, he marched against them with his force of Franks, consisting of about seven hundred knights and footmen, picked men. With these he charged on the Egyptian army, but God gave the victory to the Egyptians against his broken faction, and they killed most of his knights and foot-soldiers. He himself fled to Ramla with three followers. The Egyptians pursued and surrounded him, but he disguised himself and succeeded in eluding their vigilance, made for Yāfā, and got away from them. During the pursuit, he had hidden in a brake of canes, which was set on fire, and the fire singed part of his body, but he escaped from it and reached Yāfā. His companions were put to the sword, and all his men and champions who were captured in Ramla were killed or made prisoner, and carried off to Egypt at the end of Rajab. At this time, some Frankish vessels arrived, about forty in all, laden with men and goods, and it was reported that they had been storm-tossed and driven about by changing winds, so that most of them were lost and only a few were saved.

15th October, 1102, to 4th October, 1103

In this year the king Shams al-Mulūk Duqāq and Zahīr al-Dīn Atābek left Damascus with the 'askar, and making for al-Rahba, encamped before it and blockaded its inhabitants, cutting off all means of provisioning from them. The blockade caused such distress that the resident in the town was compelled to sue for quarter for himself and the inhabitants. They were promised safety and the town was delivered up to the king after severe fighting and prolonged warfare in Latter Jumādā (March, 1103). He placed a garrison in it and appointed a reliable officer to guard it, and having settled the affairs of its inhabitants, he set out thence on Friday the 22nd of the same month (3rd April) on his return journey to Damascus.

In this year also news was received from Hims that its lord, the amīr Janāh al-Dawla Husain Atābek, on descending from the citadel to the mosque for the Friday prayer, surrounded by his principal officers with full armour, and occupying his place of prayer, according to custom, was set upon by three Persians belonging to the Bātinīya. They were accompanied by a shaikh, to whom they owed allegiance and obedience, and all of them were dressed in the garb of ascetics. When the shaikh gave the signal they attacked the amīr with their knives and killed both him and a number of his officers. There were in the mosque at the time ten Sūfīs, Persians and others; they were suspected of complicity in the crime, and were straightway executed in cold blood, every man of them, although they were innocent. The people of Hims were greatly perturbed at this event, and at once dispersed in panic. Most of the Turks amongst the inhabitants fled to Damascus, and everything fell into confusion. The townsfolk then wrote to the king

Shams al-Mulūk at Damascus, begging him to send an officer to take over the town and be responsible for its defence, before the news reached the Franks and their covetous desires extended to it. The king Shams al-Mulūk and Zahīr al-Dīn Atābek thereupon set out with the 'askar from Damascus, reached Hims, took possession of it, and occupied the citadel. At the same time the Franks arrived at Hims and encamped at al-Rastan, with the intention of cutting off and besieging the town, but on learning what had taken place, they kept at a discreet distance and eventually withdrew.

Now the person known as al-Hakim al-Munajjim the Bātinī, a number of the entourage of the king Fakhr al-Mulūk Rudwān, lord of Aleppo, was the first to profess the doctrines of the Bātinīya in Aleppo and Syria, and it was he who commissioned the three men to kill Janāh al-Dawla at Hims. The news of his death arrived fourteen days after this event.

3 FROM *Beha-ēd-Din*

THE LIFE OF SALADIN (1137–1193)

The mood of this extremely flattering biography of Saladin is quite different from that of the earlier Damascus Chronicle, reflecting a new anti-Frankish militancy in Moslem Syria and Palestine during the late twelfth century. Saladin, whose piety, love of justice, generosity, valor, and politeness were especially noted by his biographer, proved to be the ideal leader for such a society. Nevertheless the careful reader should note the narrowness of Saladin's Moslem culture, which caused him to distrust philosophy and philosophers and to persecute Islamic religious leaders whose opinions were unorthodox. This narrowness is in contrast to the very different attitudes of the somewhat later Frederick II of Sicily, whom we shall examine in Selection 4. It shows how Islamic civilization, in closing ranks against Western Europeans in Syria, had lost some of its former breadth.

BIRTH OF SALÂH ED-DÎN. HIS GOOD QUALITIES, HIS CHARACTER, AND NATURAL DISPOSITION

I learn from the lips of certain persons worthy of credence, who had made inquiries concerning the date of the birth of Salâh

SOURCE. Beha-ēd-Din, *The Life of Saladin* (London: Palestine Pilgrim's Text Society, 1897), pp. 4–33, 38–43.

ed-Dîn, in order to construct the horoscope of this prince according to the rules of astrology, that he was born in the course of the year 532 (A.D. 1137–1138), in the citadel of Tekrit, where his father, Ayûb, son of Shâdhi, discharged his duties as Governor. Ayûb was an honourable, generous, and good man. He was born at Dovîn. Circumstances afterwards obliged him to leave Tekrît, and he betook himself to Mosul, taking his son with him. Here he remained until his son had grown up. Ayûb and his brother, Asad ed-Dîn Shîrkûh, were held in the high esteem by the Atabeg Zenghi (Prince of Mosul). Proceeding afterwards into Syria, Ayûb obtained the government of B'albek, and dwelt for some time in that place. His son, who had accompanied him, entered upon his first service under his direction. Brought up in his father's bosom, and nourished on the lofty principles which his father set before him, he soon showed signs of the good fortune which was always to accompany him, and gave evidence of a spirit born to command. El-Melek el-'Adel Nûr ed-Dîn Mahmûd, son of Zenghi, bestowed upon him advancement, and, as a mark of his confidence and high esteem, attached him to his service, and admitted him to the number of his friends. The higher Salâh ed-Dîn rose in degree, the more apparent became qualities which entitled him to a still more exalted rank. This state of things continued until his uncle, Asad ed-Dîn Shîrkûh, started upon the Egyptian expedition. Later, in a more suitable place, we will give a detailed account of this expedition, with all particulars.

WHAT I HAVE OBSERVED OF SALÂH ED-DÎN'S ATTACHMENT TO THE PRINCIPLES OF RELIGION, AND HIS RESPECT FOR EVERY PART OF THE HOLY LAW

In our collection of authentic traditions stands the following saying of the Holy Prophet: "Islâm is built upon five columns: confession of the unity of God, the regular performance of prayer, payment of the tenth (tithe) in charity, the fast of the month Ramadân, and pilgrimage to the Holy House of God (Mecca)."

Salâh ed-Dîn—may God be merciful to him!—truly believed in the doctrines of the faith, and often recited prayers in praise of God. He had accepted the dogmas of religion upon demonstrable proofs, the result of his conversations with the most learned doctors and the most eminent jurisconsults. In these arguments he acquired knowledge that enabled him to speak to the purpose when a discussion took place in his presence, although he did not employ the technical language of the lawyers. These conversations confirmed him in a true faith, which remained undisturbed by any doubt, and, in his case, prevented the arrow of speculation from overshooting the mark, and striking at last on doubt and infidelity.

The learned doctor Kotb ed-Dî en-Nisabûri had composed an exposition of Islâm for the benefit of this prince, containing all that was necessary for him to know. As he was much pleased with this treatise, he made his younger sons learn it by heart, so that good doctrine might be established in their souls from their tenderest years. I have myself seen him take this book and read it aloud to his children, after they had committed its contents to memory.

As to prayer, he was always regular in his attendance at the public service (on Fridays), and he said one day that for several years he had never failed in this duty. When he was ill, he used to send for the Imâm alone, and forcing himself to keep on his feet, would recite the Friday prayers. He recited the unusual prayers regularly, and, if he woke during the night, said a prayer. If he did not wake, he used to pray before the morning prayer. As long as consciousness lasted, he never failed to say his prayers. I saw him perform this duty regularly during his last illness, and he discontinued it only during the three days in which his mind was wandering. When he was travelling, he used to get down from his horse at the appointed hours to pray.

Let us speak of his tenth in charity. The sum of money he left at his death was not large enough to be submitted to this tax; his private charities had absorbed everything. He who had possessed such abundant wealth left in his treasury, when he died, but seven-and-forty Nâsri dirhems, and a single Tyrian gold piece. He left neither goods, nor house, nor real estate, neither garden, nor village, nor cultivated land, nor any other species of property.

Let us pass to the fast of the month Ramadân. Several of these fasts remained to be fulfilled, as he had not observed them in consequence of his frequent illnesses. It was the duty of el-Kâdi el-Fâdel to keep an account of the numbers of these days. The prince —may God have mercy on him!—was in the last year of his life, and was dwelling at Jerusalem, when he began to make reparation for the fasts he had omitted. He then fasted for a period exceeding the ordinary month, for he had still a fast of two Ramadâns to keep, which he had been prevented from observing by constant disorders of the body, and the continual cares of the Holy War. Fasting did

not suit his health; but thus, by the inspiration of God, he undertook to repair his omissions during that year. It fell to me to keep
account of the days, for the Kâdi was absent. It was useless for his
physician to disapprove of what he was doing. The prince would
not listen to him, and said, "I do not know what may happen." It
seems as though God had inspired Salâh ed-Dîn to save his
responsibility by paying his debt, and so he continued to fast until
the days were wholly accomplished.

Let us now speak of the pilgrimage. He always intended to perform it, and, above all, in the last year of his life. He had made up
his mind, and given orders for the necessary preparations to be
made. We had collected provisions for the journey, and all was
ready for the start, when he decided to postpone the pilgrimage till
the following year on account of want of time and lack of money
sufficient for one of his high rank. But God decreed as He did
decree. What I have related on that subject is a thing known to all
the world.

Salâh ed-Dîn was very fond of hearing the Kurân read, and he
used to argue with the Imâm. This man had to be master of all
knowledge connected with the text of the Kurân, and to know the
book by heart. When the prince passed the night in the alcove (of his
tent), he used to charge the man on guard to read him two, three,
or four sections. When he gave public audiences, he would have
from one to twenty verses, and sometimes more, read by men
accustomed to do so. One day he passed a little boy who was reading the Kurân very well at his father's side, and was so pleased that
he had the boy called, and gave him some of the food set aside for
his own special use. Also he granted to him and his father part of
the produce of a certain field. His heart was humble, and full of
compassion; tears came readily into his eyes. When he was listening to the reading of the Kurân, his heart melted, and tears
generally flowed down his cheeks. He was very fond of listening to
the recital of traditions when the narrator could trace each tradition that he related to its source, and when he was learned in such
lore. If one of the doctors visited the court, he received him personally, and made those of his sons who happened to be present as
well as the memlûks on duty, listen to the traditions recited. He
would order all those who were present to be seated during the
narration, as a sign of respect. If any of the doctors of traditionary
lore were such characters as do not frequent the gates of Sultans,
and are unwilling to present themselves in such places, Salâh

ed-Dîn would go himself to seek them out and listen to them. When he was at Alexandria, he often visited Hâfiz el-Isfahâni, and learnt from him a great number of traditions. He himself was fond of reading traditions, so he used to make me come into his private chamber, and there, surrounded by books of traditions which he had had collected, he would begin to read; and whenever he came to a tradition containing an instructive passage, he was so touched that the tears came into his eyes.

He showed the greatest zeal in his observance of the precepts of religion, openly maintaining his belief in the resurrection of the bodies of the just in Paradise, and of the wicked in Hell. He believed steadfastly in all the teaching of the Divine Law, accepting its doctrines with an open heart. He detested philosophers, heretics, materialists, and all adversaries of orthodox religion. He even ordered his son el-Melek ez-Zâher, Prince of Aleppo—may God exalt his supporters!—to put to death a young man named Suhraverdi. He had been accused of not recognizing the ordinances of the law, and of paying no regard to the doctrines of the faith. Ez-Zâher, having sent this man to prison, reported what had passed to his father, and at Salâh ed-Dîn's command had him executed, and his body hung upon a cross for several days.

Having perfect trust in God, he looked upon Him as his great support, and turned ever to Him. I will give an instance of this which I myself witnessed. The Franks—may God confound them! —had pitched their camp at Beit-Nûba, a place situated about a day's journey from Jerusalem. The Sultan occupied this city, after having surrounded the enemy with out-posts, and sent out men to spy and watch all their movements. He received constant news of the Franks, and of their fixed determination to come up to the Holy City and lay siege to it. As this struck great terror among the Moslems, he called his emirs together, informed them of the calamity which threatened the faithful, and submitted to them whether it was right to remain in the city. They appeared, one and all, of good courage, but their real sentiments were very different from those which they expressed. They declared unanimously that the Sultan's presence in Jerusalem would be of no advantage, and might, indeed, endanger Islâm; that they themselves would remain there, while he went out with a body of men to surround the Franks, as had been done at Acre. At the head of this army, he was to keep the enemy narrowly hemmed in, and cut off their supplies of provisions; meanwhile, they would hold the city and repel attacks. The council having broken up, the Sultan forthwith determined to hold the city, knowing full well that otherwise no one would remain there. After the emirs had left to return to their houses, a messenger came from them to the Sultan to inform him that they would not remain in Jerusalem, unless he left at their head either his brother el-Melek el-'Âdel, or one of his own sons. He felt that this communication meant that they did not intend to remain in the city, and his heart was sorely oppressed, and he knew not what to decide. On this same night, which was the eve of Friday, I was on duty in his chamber, having to stay there from evening until dawn. It was in the rainy season, and with us two there was no third but God. We made plans, and discussed the consequences of each plan; but at last I grew concerned for him, seeing him so overwhelmed with despair, and I began to fear for his health. So I begged him to lie down on his bed, and sleep a little if possible. He replied: "You must be sleepy, too," then he rose (to withdraw). Passing into my house, I busied myself with some private affairs until dawn, when the summons to prayer sounded. As I usually said the morning-prayer with him, I went into his chamber, where I found him washing. "I have not slept a single moment," he said. I replied that I knew it. "How?" he asked. I answered, "Because I have not slept myself, not having had the time." We then said our prayers, after which we sat down to what we had to do. At last I said: "I have an idea that, I believe, is a good one, please God!" "What is it?" he asked. I replied: "Support is from God, turn to Him and trust in His goodness, and you will be delivered out of this affliction." "And what shall we do?" he inquired. I answered: "To-day is Friday; your Highness will perform a ceremonial ablution before going this afternoon to the Aksa; you will say your prayer as usual in the holy place of the Prophet's night journey. You will charge a confidential servant to give alms in secret; then you will say a prayer of two rak'a after the azān and before the ikâma, and whilst you remain prostrate, you will call upon God for help. We have a credible tradition on this subject. Your Highness will say within yourself: *Oh God! all earthly means that I have employed, for the defence of religion, now fail me. There remains for me no resource but to seek support in Thee, to put myself in Thy hand, and to trust myself to Thy goodness. Upon Thee alone do I count, Thou art the best of guardians.* Rest assured that God is too generous to reject your appeal." He did exactly as I had advised, and I prayed by his side as usual. Whilst he said the two rak'a between the azân and the ikâma, his body prostrate, I saw the tears fall on to his grizzling beard, and then on to the prayer-carpet; but I did not hear what he had said. Before we had reached the end of the day a dispatch arrived in which 'Izz ed-Dîn Jurdîk, who was then in command of the advanced guard, informed us that a great disturbance reigned amongst the Franks; that their men had this day mounted their horses and betaken themselves to the plain; that they had halted there until noon, and then all at once returned to their camp. Early on Saturday a second dispatch arrived with the same news. During the day a spy came in and reported that discord was rampant amongst the Franks, the king of France having declared that they must absolutely lay siege to Jerusalem, whilst the king of England and his supporters were unwilling to risk the Christian cause by throwing their troops into a mountainous country, where their water-supply would be entirely cut off, for the Sultan had destroyed all the wells round the city. Also that their chiefs had gone out (from the camp) to hold a council in their usual manner, for it is their custom, when it is a question of war, to take counsel together on horseback. Also that they had agreed to refer the point to the consideration of ten persons whom they had chosen from amongst themselves, and to abide by their decision. On Monday morning a messenger came to announce that the enemy had struck their camp, and were marching towards Ramla. This was an instance of the Sultan's great trust in God. I myself was a witness of it.

. . . . .

HIS VALOUR AND INTREPIDITY—MAY GOD HALLOW HIS SOUL!

The Holy Prophet is reported to have said: "God loves bravery, even (if displayed) only in killing a serpent." The Sultan was bravest among the brave; he was distinguished by his energy of soul, his vigour of character, and his intrepidity. I have seen him take up his position immediately in front of a large body of Franks, who were every moment being increased and relieved, and the sight (of this danger) only strengthened his courage and nerve. One evening there came up more than seventy of the enemy's ships; it took me the whole of the time between the 'Asr prayer and the prayer at sunset to count them; but their appearance only served to inspirit him anew. On another occasion, at the commencement of the rainy season, he gave leave to his troops, and remained himself, attended by very few men, in the face of a strong force of the enemy. On the day when peace was concluded, Bâliân, son of Bârizân, one of the chief princes of the coast, was seated before the Sultan, and I inquired of him what was the number of their troops. I received this answer through the interpreter: "When the Lord of Sidon" (another of their chiefs, and one of the most intelligent among them) "and I left Tyre to join our army (at the siege of Acre), and when we sighted them from the top of the hill, we tried to guess as nearly as we could the number of those engaged. The Lord of Sidon said there were five hundred thousand; I said six hundred thousand." I then asked him how many they had lost, and he replied: "Nearly a hundred thousand on the field of battle; but God alone knows the numbers of those who have died from sickness, or who have been drowned." And of all this multitude but a very small number ever returned to their native land.

When we were close upon the enemy, the Sultan insisted on making a reconnaissance round their army once or twice every day. In the height of the fighting he used to pass between the two lines of battle, accompanied by a young page, who led his horse. He would make his way in front of his own troops from the right wing to the left, intent on the marshalling of his battalions, calling them up to the front, and stationing them in positions which he deemed advantageous to command the enemy or to approach them. On one occasion, whilst standing between the two armies, he ordered that some traditions should be read to him. It is a fact. I told him that traditions could be read in all important places, but that there was no instance of its having been done between two armies. I added that if his Highness would like such a thing told of him, it would be fine. He listened to this. A volume was brought, and someone who was present, and had studied the book, read to him from it. Meanwhile, we remained on horseback, sometimes walking up and down, sometimes standing still, but all the while on the ground between the two armies.

. . . . .

In the year 583 (A.D. 1187), at the battle of Haṭṭîn—a famous day's fight of which, please God, we shall speak in its proper place—Prince Arnât (Renaud de Chatillon), Lord of el-Kerak, and the king of the Franks of the sea-coast, were both taken prisoners, and the Sultan commanded them to be brought before him. This accursed

Arnât was a great infidel, and a very strong man. On one occasion, when there was a truce between the Moslems and the Franks, he treacherously attacked and carried off a caravan that passed through his territory, coming from Egypt. He seized these people, put them to torture, and put some of them in grain-pits, and imprisoned some in narrow cells. When they objected that there was a truce between the two peoples, he replied: "Ask your Muhammad to deliver you." The Sultan, to whom these words were reported, took an oath to slay the infidel with his own hand, if God should ever place him in his power. The day of the battle of Hattîn God delivered this man into the hands of the Sultan, and he resolved at once to slay him, that he might fulfil his oath. He commanded him to be brought before him, together with the king. The latter complained of thirst, and the Sultan ordered a cup of sherbert to be given to him. The king, having drunk some of it, handed the cup to Arnât, whereupon the Sultan said to the interpreter: "Say to the king, 'It is you who give him drink, but I give him neither to drink nor to eat.' " By these words he wished it to be understood that honour forbade him to harm any man who had tasted his hospitality. He then struck him on the neck with his own hand, to fulfil the vow he had made. After this, when he had taken Acre, he delivered all the prisoners, to the number of about four thousand, from their wretched durance, and sent them back to their own country and their homes, giving each of them a sum of money for the expenses of his journey. This is what I have been told by many persons, for I was not present myself when it took place.

4 FROM   *Lionel Allshorn*
THE LIFE OF FREDERICK II OF SICILY

*This view of the character and accomplishments of a great thirteenth-century
Western ruler shows the way in which Moslem civilization could merge with that of
Western Europe and help produce the fascinating Frederick, or "Stupor Mundi" as
he was called by some contemporaries. Many historians would argue that what is
written here of Frederick was equally true of his predecessor, Roger II of Sicily, a
century earlier. Roger II's court and administration at Palermo showed the same
sensitivity to Moslem practices and Islamic culture as Frederick II's. It is not sur-
prising that both monarchs helped popularize Moslem intellectual accomplishments
and art in the Europe of the twelfth and thirteenth centuries.*

The monk of St. Albans, in bestowing upon Frederick the title of
"the wonder of the world," deems it unnecessary to enlarge upon
that title by comment and explanation. We may take it that he is but
recording the universal opinion of his age. The magnificent and un-
paralleled figure of the Roman Emperor had excited in his generation a sentiment of wonder, and whether men marvelled at him with
admiration or deprecation, to friend and enemy alike he was a being
whose career and personality evoked surpassing interest and pro-
found surprise.

We may conceive easily enough how this sentiment had arisen.
The sudden change in his fortunes, which in his youth had elevated
him from the position of a powerless King to that of the first
monarch of Christendom, had no doubt attracted considerable
attention; and from henceforth, by virtue of his high office, he could
no longer remain in obscurity. But it was the circumstances of his
Crusade that first made him the cynosure of all eyes. His abortive
embarkation for the Holy Land and the excommunication which
had been immediately launched against him formed a dramatic pre-
lude. His subsequent departure in defiance of the ban of the Church

SOURCE, Lionel Allshorn, *Stupor Mundi: The Life and Times of Frederick II, Emperor
of the Romans, King of Sicily and Jerusalem, 1194–1250* (London: Martin Secker &
Warburg Ltd., 1912), pp. 281–295. Reprinted by permission of the publisher.

and the attack which the enraged Pope had made upon his dominions, offered to Europe the strange spectacle of an Emperor leading a Crusade who was himself the object of a Crusade. The extraordinary success which he had obtained by peaceful means, in spite of the persistent antagonism of the Papal party, had earned him the admiring gratitude of Christendom; while at the same time his friendly intercourse with the Sultan and his broad-minded attitude towards the Infidels had mingled with that admiration an emotion of shocked amazement.

He had returned to his European dominions with his dignity enhanced by the acquisition of the Crown of Jerusalem, and had wrested from the Pope the revocation of the sentence of excommunication. Men had then gradually become informed of his astonishing mental attainments, had learnt of how he could discourse with Jews, Arabians, Frenchmen, Italians and Germans in their own tongues, of how he had mastered the learning of Greece and Rome, of how he could meet on terms of equality, if not of superiority, with the greatest scholars of his age in every branch of knowledge. The elegance and magnificence of his Court, its Oriental splendour and its cosmopolitan hospitality, had been noised abroad. His maintenance of a harem, though it would have passed unnoticed had he been merely the King of Sicily, became a glaring defiance of propriety in one who was the chief monarch of Christendom: men whispered in horrified undertones that he was even suspected of indulging in carnal pleasures with Infidel women. He had ignored the prejudices of his day by planting a colony of Saracens in the very heart of his Kingdom and by employing them as his soldiers. He had flouted religious bigotry by allowing Greeks, Jews and Infidels to worship as they pleased. He was even said to have derided the Immaculate Conception, to have placed Christ on a level with Moses and Mahomet, to have become almost a Saracen himself in belief and in manner of life.

. . . . .

Thus around his name there had gathered a glamour of strangeness and splendour, of genius soaring to perilous questionings of eternal truths, of unbreakable resolution and of unconquerable pride. To his ardent supporters he had become the new Messiah, to his frenzied enemies the Antichrist. To those who stood outside the immediate fury of the strife he was a being beyond the common range of human experience and comprehension. He was the dominating spirit of his age, the supreme centre of interest and wonder, *stupor mundi et immutator mirabilis.*

. . . . .

He was entirely Oriental in his sexual conduct. He may have been profoundly attached to Bianca Lancia, or to one of his legitimate wives, but their position was only that of the favoured Sultana: they never enjoyed the monopoly of his embraces. He was not a hunter of women: surrounded by a bevy of complaisant beauties who existed solely for his own pleasure, the wives of his subjects were safe from his regards. Yet this Orientalism, though less mischievous than the roving amorousness of a Charles the Second, is less easy to condone. It is sensuality without sentiment, devoid of the glamour of romance; a mere satisfaction of erotic impulse or bodily appetite rather than ardent passion or impetuous desire. It is unforgivable in one of his enlightened mind. We may concede that his morality was not lower than that of his age; but we cannot deny that he transgressed the bounds of that licence which, if we would be tolerant, we must regard as the peculiar privilege of princes.

To the men of his own country these faults in Frederick's character were ordinary enough: they were the sins that might be laid to the charge of any ruler, great or small, in Mediæval Italy. But there was an offence which, in the eyes of a superstitious age, was far more grievous than these. It is not for lewdness or cruelty or treachery that Dante consigns Frederick to hell, but for unbelief. The poet, Imperialist though he is, cannot ignore the accusation which was made against the Emperor by his enemies, which was confirmed by his own hasty and scornful words. Frederick is an "illustrious hero," his character is "of nobility and righteousness"; but nevertheless, because he doubted the eternal truths, his portion is among the heresiarchs in hell.

How far the popular impression of his scepticism was correct it is, of course, impossible to determine. It is unlikely that he was an atheist, for when he realized that the hand of death was upon him, he said, "The will of God be done." We may believe, however, that a mind of such broad and catholic culture could not but revolt against the narrow dogma of the Church: that mingling in himself the civilization of both Christendom and Mohammedanism, he viewed the two religions with a certain detachment, and regarded with impatience the claims of either to exclusive infallibility: that to his scientific and enquiring mind any sharply defined doctrine would be unacceptable, especially when it contained so large an element of superstition as the religious belief of his day. Unprovoked by the Papal enmity, he might have veiled his opinions in discreet silence; but harassed beyond measure by an unjust persecution, he was occasionally stung into deriding the religion of which his arch enemy was the earthly head.

. . . . .

It is always more easy to define the vices of a man than his virtues. The vices of Frederick can be exemplified by material things, his licentiousness by the harem that he maintained for his pleasure, his cruelty by the leaden cope, said to be his own invention, under the weight of which his victims slowly wearied to death. For his great qualities we must look with a wider view, must envisage his whole life. We must note that fine pride which enabled him to resist the allurements of a life of peacefulness and cultured ease, and to end his days in ceaseless warfare and toil. We must regard the all-powerful intellect, the mind freed from the trammels of religious bigotry, the enlightened measures for the prosperity and mental elevation of his people. How far in him the good exceeded the evil, the light triumphed over the darkness, may be gathered from the men who were his friends. The saintly Louis of France found in him more righteousness than in the Vicar of Christ. Hermann von Salza, a man of blameless life and lofty reputation, was his loyal friend and trusty servant as long as he lived. Berard, the Archbishop of Palermo, against whose name there was no breath of calumny, clung to his side through excommunication and deposition, never denied to him the sacred offices forbidden by the Pope, absolved him on his deathbed and buried him with the full rites of the Church. Even that Pope who summoned in Charles of Anjou to extirpate his house could call him "the noble Frederick" and extol his government of the Kingdom.

5 FROM *J. H. Kramers*
ISLAMIC GEOGRAPHY AND COMMERCE

*This article first appeared almost forty years ago. Although the author's failure to
deal adequately with the commerce of the Mediterranean, as it affected the Islamic
world, makes his analysis somewhat inadequate, it still remains the best overall treatment of this difficult subject. It demonstrates the crucial role that Islamic merchants
played in linking China and India with the West, and it shows how Moslem geographers pioneered a relatively novel view of the world as a whole. Finally, it enables
us to appreciate the role of the medieval Arabs in transmitting to the West new plants
and manufacturing processes, and better methods of carrying on business.*

Were we to draw a map of the political condition of Europe,
Africa, and western Asia about the middle of the tenth century of
our era, we should see that by far the greater part of that "inhabited
world", which the Greeks called the "oikoumene", was occupied by
countries possessed of an Islamic government and an Islamic
civilization. They no longer constituted a strict political unity, but
they were connected by such strong ties of common religion and
culture that their inhabitants—and not only their Muhammadan
inhabitants—felt themselves citizens of one vast empire, of which
Mecca was the religious, and Baghdād the cultural and political
centre. This vast empire had grown in the three foregoing centuries
from a series of conquests that started originally from Medina.
Arabia was its centre. To the west it comprised Egypt with the
entire northern coast of Africa, including the Atlantic coast as far
as the Anti-Atlas and, further, nearly the whole of Spain (with the
exception of Asturia), and the islands of Sicily and Crete. Sardinia
and Cyprus, too, were constantly exposed to Muhammadan attacks;
so was also the southern Italian coast, where some towns, like Bari,
were actually under Islamic rule, while others, like Amalfi, belonged
to its sphere of influence. To the north of Arabia, Syria with Armenia
and the south-east of the Caucasus belonged to the permanent
possessions of Islam; and, farther to the east, Mesopotamia with

SOURCE. J. H. Kramers, "Geography and Commerce," in Sir Thomas Arnold and
Alfred Guillaume, eds., *The Legacy of Islam* (Oxford: The Clarendon Press, 1931),
pp. 79–106. Reprinted by permission of the publisher.

'Irāq, followed by the whole of the territory of modern Persia with Afghanistan. Northward of these countries, again, Transoxania belonged to Islam, including in the west the delta region of Khwārizm, and, in the east, the valley and the mountains of Farghâna. The Indus has been crossed already in the eighth century; the regions on its lower course belonged, with Sind, to the Islamic Empire. Only in the southward direction did the territorial extension of Islam in Africa scarcely exceed the latitude of Aswān in Egypt.

"The length of the Empire of Islam in our days extends from the limits of Farghāna, passing through Khurāsān, al-Jibāl (Media), 'Irāq and Arabia as far as the coast of Yaman, which is a journey of about four months; its breadth begins from the country of the Rūm (the Byzantine Empire), passing through Syria, Mesopotamia, 'Irāq, Fārs and Kirmān, as far as the territory of al-Mansūra on the shore of the sea of Fārs (the Indian Ocean), which is about four months' travelling. In the previous statement of the length of Islam I have omitted the frontier of the Maghrib (northern Africa) and Andalus (Spain), because it is like the sleeve of a garment. To the east and the west of the Maghrib there is no Islam. If one goes, however, beyond Egypt into the country of the Maghrib, the lands of the Sūdān (the Black) lie to the south of the Maghrib and, to its north, the Sea of Rūm (the Mediterranean) and next the territory of Rūm."

These are the words of the geographer Ibn Hauqal, writing about A.D. 975.

Although the regions enumerated above do not coincide at all with, and are even smaller than, the countries now inhabited by a Muhammadan population, the fact that they constituted not only a religious but also a politically powerful block, brought together and kept together by force of arms, enabled them to hold the position of a strong central power in the world then known.

If we consider, on the other hand, the geographical and political conditions of the Christian European world of those days, we immediately realize to what extent in reality the latter must have been dependent on the huge Islamic Empire. To the south the Mediterranean, at that time under the domination of the rulers of the Muhammadan shores, formed an insurmountable barrier; to the east the Byzantine Empire stood face to face with Islam in Armenia; the northern Caucasus and eastern Europe were the home of half-civilized nations that were at least as much under

Muhammadan as under Christian influence. Only in the north of Europe the heathen Northmen were at the beginning of their powerful extension, which was largely to contribute, in the twelfth century, to the annihilation of the political and economic hegemony of Islam.

The relative geographical position of the pilgrimage centres of the two rival religions was quite different. Jerusalem, the ideal religious centre of Christian Europe, had since A.D. 638 been under the control of the Muhammadans, but the Muhammadan conquest had not put an end to the pilgrimages undertaken by European Christians to the Holy Sepulchre. The first pilgrims of whose travels accounts have come down to us, were the Frank Arculf (c. 680), the Saxon Willibald (c, 725) and a certain Bernard, who started c. 870 from Rome on a pilgrimage. No doubt they were not the only ones that contributed to the maintenance of knowledge about the countries conquered by Islam. The relations of the Christians in the Byzantine Empire with their co-religionists in Egypt, Syria, and Mesopotamia must have been very important in this respect.

In the Islamic world matters were quite different. Mecca, the centre of pilgrimage, occupied a central geographical position in Islam itself. The pilgrimage or "hajj" to Allah's house was one of the five "pillars of Islam," according to the Sacred Law, and Muhammadans from all parts of the Islamic Empire met at that place. So the "hajj" became not only a powerful factor in promoting religious unity, but it also materially assisted in strengthening the ties of commerce between all Muhammadan countries, and disseminated among Muhammadans a fairly good knowledge of all parts of their world. To the "hajj" was due the compilation of a number of itineraries, in which the stations and stages of the roads leading from different countries to Mecca were indicated. There was, however, a great ignorance of, and lack of interest in, the non-Muhammadan parts of the known world.

Nearly a millennium has passed since the cultural horizon of Christian Europe was bounded in nearly all directions by Islam. In the meantime Europe has circumnavigated and pierced the barriers that separated it from the southern and eastern parts of the known world, not to speak of the unknown world. Europe owes much to its own force and initiative, but it has also largely profited by the knowledge and the experience of those who were at one time the masters of the world. Therefore Europe ought to look upon them as its cultural ancestors in the domain of geographical knowledge, of discovery, and of world trade. The influence which Islam has exercised on our modern civilization in these spheres of action can be seen in the many terms of Arabic origin which are to be found in the vocabulary of trade and navigation. The measure of this influence can only be proved by studying the historical development of the domain over which our actual geographical knowledge extends. For modern geography is a science so positive and independent of tradition that it all but excludes the more or less correct views of former ages; I say "all but," for it is only just to remember the fact that, when Jaubert in 1840 edited his French translation of Idrīsī, it was thought not unlikely that this edition might increase geographical knowledge of the world, and especially of Africa.

. . . . .

Islamic navigation had already reached its widest extent in the ninth century. But, while navigation on the Indian Ocean derived its chief importance from the commercial relations with the non-Islamic coasts of Asia and Africa, commercial navigation in the Mediterranean was limited to the parts under Muhammadan rule, the relations with Christian ports being of a military and predatory character.

The Indian Ocean, consequently, was the only field of great enterprise. Its base was the Persian Gulf, where ports like Sīrāf and Basra, with its suburb al-Ubulla, and those on the Omān coast had been, even in pre-Islamic times, very important centres of trade and navigation. The coming of Islam, however, and especially the establishment of its political centre in 'Irāq, encouraged the spirit of enterprise. About the middle of the tenth century Muhammadan ships had already reached the Chinese town of Khanfu, now Canton. There was then a considerable Islamic colony in that town, which had become an emporium of the trade with China. From here some Muhammadan traders and sailors went even farther north, and it is probable that they knew Corea and Japan. This early commercial prosperity seems to have been brought to an end in 878 by certain disturbances, in which the port of Khanfu was destroyed. From that time regular navigation did not extend farther than a town which the Arabic authors call Kala, famed especially for its tin mines, the position of which must be sought on the western coast of Malacca. Kala was politically dependent on the ruler of Zābaj, which name is the early Arabic rendering of the name Java. But at that time

Zābaj stood in the first place for Sumatra, and particularly for the centre of the then flourishing empire of Shrivijaya; with these regions trading connexions existed. It appears from such authors as Ibn Rusta (c. 900), Sulaimān (c. 850) and his continuator Abū Zaid (c. 950) that the Muhammadan navigators were quite at home in those seas, though the texts do not give a very clear account of the sea-routes which were followed. The ships of Islam kept up an equally lively traffic with the ports of Ceylon (Sarandīb) and with the west coast of India; a prosperous Arabic colony inhabited the town of Saimūr in the neighbourhood of Bombay. Daibul, situated in Sind on Muhammadan territory, was an important emporium for these regions. On the eastern coast of Africa—where, on the whole, trade was less important—they reached, in the beginning of the tenth century, the country of Sufāla, known for its gold. This region was on the African coast, opposite Madagascar, and the island itself was known to the Muhammadans as the isle of Wāqwāq. Now the authors knew also another Wāqwāq, which was opposite China, and the description of which seems best to answer to that of Japan. The result was, of course, a fatal confusion in the accounts given in geographical texts, caused, no doubt, by the geographical dogma that the east coast of Africa ran in an eastern direction to reach, somewhere in the neighbourhood of China, the mouth of the "sea of Fārs." The knowledge of the sea-captains was not hampered by traditional views, as has been shown; stories of their voyages are very popular in Arabic literature and were soon invested with a romantic hue which has survived in the well-known tales of Sindbād the Sailor in the *Arabian Nights*.

The age-long seafaring tradition which centres in the Persian Gulf prepared the way for the nations that afterwards sailed and ruled those waters: Portuguese, Turks, British, and Dutch. When Vasco de Gama, after his circumnavigation of Africa in 1498, had reached Malindi on the east coast of Africa, it was an Arab pilot that showed him the way to India. According to Portuguese sources, this pilot was in possession of a very good sea-map and of other maritime instruments. Arabic sources of that time also knew the story; they state that the pilot, whom they knew under the name of Aḥmad ibn Mājid, could only be induced to show the way to the Portuguese after having been made drunk. This probably fictitious story shows that the Muhammadans fully realized the far-reaching consequences of the coming of the Portuguese. The same Aḥmad ibn Mājid is also known as the writer of a sailing-manual for the

Indian Ocean, the Red Sea, the Persian Gulf, the South China Sea, and the East-Indian archipelago. According to a statement of Sir R. F. Burton it even seems that Ibn Mājid was venerated in the past century on the African coast as the inventor of the compass.

The idea of piercing the isthmus of Suez is ascribed to some of the earlier Abbasid caliphs; it was never realized, however, and since the Crusades such an enterprise was justly considered a great danger to Islam. Islamic navigation in the Mediterranean has therefore always been isolated from that in the Eastern waters: trade in the Mediterranean was restricted to Muhammadan ports. Commercial relations with Christian countries were strongly opposed, both from the Islamic side—as early as the Caliph Omar—and from the Christian side. The result was the decay of the port of Alexandria and the ruin of many other ancient seaports. Now Tunis became the new centre of the considerable traffic between north African and Spanish ports. Towards Christians Muhammadan navigators were often nothing but pirates, but it is only just to say that the same thing is true of Christian navigators.

From the beginning of the Crusades the Mediterranean ceased to be almost the exclusive domain of Islamic navigation. Islam had lost a great part of Spain, the island of Sicily, and its hold on the Italian coast; at the same time the Italian seaports of Genoa and Pisa began to develop. The traveller Ibn Jubair, in 1192, made use of a Christian ship to go from Ceuta to Alexandria. In practice this transition of maritime hegemony was much less violent. It only meant that the Christians, who had navigated before as sailors or slaves under Muslim control, now fully emancipated themselves and sailed and traded on their own account. The modern international maritime vocabulary contains not a few words of Arabic origin, which show the former Muhammadan supremacy on these seas, such words for example as admiral, cable, average, shallop (sloop), barque, and, in the maritime language of the Indian Ocean, monsoon.

Mention has already been made of the compass in connexion with the pilot Ibn Mājid. This man himself supposes in his work that the inventor of the compass was King David. But it cannot even be proved that the Muhammadans were acquainted with this instrument at an earlier date than the Christians. It may be true that the Chinese knew this instrument and its use in the second century and that they transmitted it to the West. But the first indubitable indication that Islamic sea-captains knew the compass is found in an author of 1282, and this is about the same time that a knowledge of it can be traced in France and Italy. Some terms of oriental but not Arabic provenance in the terminology relating to the compass make it probable that Europe received the knowledge of the qualities of the magnetic needle from the East, but it does not appear that the Muhammadans were the predecessors of the Christians. Their, in many respects, clumsy cartography makes us rather suppose that their ships could sail only in sight of the shore. So it is safer to assume that, even if the Muhammadans knew of the compass earlier than European Christians, their acquaintance with it does not go back beyond 1200 and that, soon after it became known to them, the knowledge of it was passed on to Christian navigators.

The problem connected with the appearance of the first sea-charts of the Mediterranean at the end of the thirteenth century closely resembles the problem of the compass. The oldest known portulan was probably made by the Genoese. The portulans give at once a much more exact image of the position of coasts and islands than all the earlier maps, and their construction was only made possible by the use of the compass. The portulans also show a very detailed design of the coastlines, and these details can hardly have been the work of one generation. Now we need only remember the exact description of the African coast in the work of al-Idrīsī and his predecessors Ibn Hauqal and al-Bakrī, to realize that the experience of the Islamic navigators—reflected in the geographical treatises cited above—must have contributed considerably to the composition of those prototypes of modern cartography, the oldest portulans.

By the big water-ways of Mesopotamia the Persian Gulf was linked to Baghdād, the centre of the Islamic Empire. By this means the navigation of the Indian Ocean became the instrument of a world-trade. The great merchants of Baghdād obtained in this way the silks of China and the spices and aromatics of India, different kinds of wood, coco-nuts, muscat-nuts, and the tin of Kala. All these wares found their way from Islamic countries into Europe, then deprived of all direct traffic with those countries. A part of this sea-trade did not enter the Persian Gulf, but brought the products to Aden and the Red-Sea ports of Jedda and al-Qulzum (the ancient Clysma near Suez), and, in the crusading times, to 'Aidhāb, an ancient port for pilgrim caravans which lay about opposite Jedda. From here the occidental part of the Islamic world was supplied.

By the same way came also the African products, such as ivory; these were shipped from the Ethiopian seaport of Zaila', opposite Aden.

More typical than navigation of the traffic of Islam is the overland trade by the "ship of the desert." Though, long before the appearance of Muhammad, trade caravans had crossed the steppes of Asia and Africa, we are accustomed to associate caravan trade with Islam. Even down to the last few years the Islamic peoples have not been surpassed by western civilization in the means of locomotion in the desert. The recently started motor traffic in the Syrian desert, in Arabia, in Persia, and in the Sahara, some railways in Central Asia, and the recently established air services have begun to follow the immemorial tracks of the camel. In the centuries when the Islamic Empire flourished, caravan traffic was the most common means of travelling and trading between the different Islamic countries, especially the pilgrim caravans to Mecca. At the same time there were some important overland routes that led out of the Empire, first those to India and China, secondly those to southern and central Russia and thirdly the African trade-roads. India and China could also be reached by sea; for this reason the caravan trade was not so important on this side as in other directions. The land-route to India was moreover hampered by the difficult roads in the mountains of Afghanistan. To trade with China it was necessary to pass through the regions occupied by Turkish peoples; the chief Chinese product, silk, was produced, moreover, in Persia at an early period. After the fall of the Sāmānid Empire, in the eleventh century, political conditions became still more unfavourable for the Chinese overland trade. The great revival of the Asian trade routes in the thirteenth century was not the work of Islam, but of the Mongols.

For our knowledge of the extension of Islamic trade influence in a northerly direction we can rely not only on written sources, but also on the enormous number of Muhammadan coins which have been found in different parts of Russia, Finland, Sweden, and Norway, not to mention some isolated finds in the British Isles and in Iceland. On the middle course of the Volga, in the province of Kazan, great quantities of these coins have been found, but these are far surpassed in number by the Arabic coins found in the Baltic provinces. In Scandinavia the chief finds are on the south-western coast of Sweden and the southern point of Norway. The coins belong to the period from the end of the seventh to the beginning of the eleventh century. It is very unlikely that the Islamic merchants themselves advanced so far to the north as these places, for it appears from the written Arabic sources that the country of the Volga Bulgars, on the middle course of that river, was the final goal of their trade expeditions and their embassies; the faith of Islam, too, penetrated as far as those regions at an early date. The route generally followed by trade went from Transoxania to the Delta region of Khwārizm (Khiva) at the mouth of the Oxus; the way up the Volga from its mouth was less usual. The fact, however, that the coins are found over so wide an area is a symptom of cultural influence, and proves that the Muhammadans purchased in the Bulgarian markets a good many wares from the peoples living in the north-west. Amongst these the Scandinavian Russians were the most important. We know from geographical works, principally from al-Maqdisī, what were the wares that the Islamic merchants acquired in this way: "sables, miniver, ermines, the fur of foxes, beavers, spotted hares, and goats; also wax, arrows, burch bark, high fur caps, fish glue, fish teeth, castoreum, amber, prepared horse hides, honey, hazel nuts, falcons, swords, armour, maple wood, slaves, small and big cattle." Most of the slaves come from the Slavonic peoples, whose name still bears witness to the role they played in the civilized world and especially the Islamic countries. Another way by which slaves were imported was Spain, whence they came to the Maghrib and Egypt. This last category were chiefly eunuchs destined for the Islamic harems. It is well known that the slaves of different races so imported have contributed not a little to the spreading of Islamic cultural acquisitions in Europe. Apart from this far-reaching Islamic-Bulgarian trade—of which traces have been found also in Germany—there were also commercial relations with the empire of the Khazars, by the Caspian Sea and the mouths of the Volga, where was situated Itil or Atil, the capital of the Khazars. This trade was less important for the exchange of merchandise, but the Khazar Empire, constituting a kind of buffer-state between Islam and the Byzantine Empire, furthered the transmission of many Islamic and oriental products which found their way into Christian countries.

The African overland trade was divided into an eastern and a western area; on both sides the chief import was gold. In the country of the Buja, to the east of Aswān, beyond Islamic territory, lay al-'Allāqī, the big trade-centre of the region of the gold mines, famous since ancient Egyptian times. In western Africa an active trade went on with the gold country of Ghāna, the capital of which

must have been on the Niger. The Muhammadan merchants from
Morocco, Algeria, and Tunisia travelled several months' journey
to the south and passed generally through Awdaghosht, an oasis
situated fourteen days' journey to the north of Ghāna. As a proof
of the importance of trade in those regions the geographer Ibn
Hauqal (c. 975) alleges that he saw in Awdaghosht an I.O.U. (the
Arabic word is *sakk*, from which the modern word cheque has been
derived), for an amount of 42,000 dinars, addressed to a merchant
in the town of Sijilmāsa in southern Morocco. It is even said that
in the preceding century the volume of trade had been still greater,
as there existed then a straight road connexion between the western
regions and Egypt, which road had been given up on account of
its insecurity.

In later centuries, also, Africa remained a domain where Muhammadan enterprise and missionary zeal could display their activity
without competition. The author Ibn Saʿīd, in the thirteenth
century, is very well acquainted, through the travels of Ibn Fātima,
with the Atlantic coast as far as the Senegal (which was thought to
be connected with the Niger and even to belong to the same fluvial
system as the Nile), and with the negro peoples living round Lake
Chad; on the other hand, the Muhammadans never knew the
sources of the Nile, for they only repeat the tradition of Ptolemy
on this point. Still the Europe of the Renaissance had no information except from Muhammadan sources about the interior of the
Dark Continent, for the description of Africa by the christianized
Muslim Leo Africanus in 1526 was then, and for long afterwards,
almost the only source of knowledge. The value attributed to Idrīsī
in the first half of the nineteenth century has already been pointed
out.

The trade between Islam and Christian Europe showed at first a
sharp contrast with the large commercial development previously
described. There was as good as no direct commercial intercourse.
What trade there was lay in the hands of Jewish merchants. At that
time the Jews were almost exclusively a commercial people and only
they could trade freely in both areas of civilization. Ibn Khur-
radādhbeh relates that Jewish merchants from the south of France
crossed the sea to Egypt, traversed on foot the isthmus of Suez, and
travelled by ship to India; others went overland from Ceuta to
Egypt, and from Syria to the Indus. They often visited Constantinople also. In this way the Islamic countries received from Europe
slaves—of whom mention has already been made—silks (from the

Byzantine Empire), furs, and arms, all of which came also by way
of Russia. The same traders brought to Europe musk, aloes, camphor, cinnamon, and similar products; the names betray their
oriental origin. Other routes by which oriental products could
enter Europe were the Empire of the Khazars, between the Caspian
region and Byzantium, and the half-barbaric peoples of Russia,
that kept up a lively trade with central Europe. On the Byzantine
frontier the town of Trebizond was in the tenth century an important emporium for the Islamic-Greek trade. A number of
Muhammadan merchants lived there, and the Byzantine government
profited largely by the levying of customs. There was also some
direct trade on the Spanish border.

So we may speak, in a way, of a state of mutual commercial
isolation between the Christian and the Muhammadan world. It is
true that since the eighth century Muslim travellers and traders are
to be found in Italian towns and in Constantinople, but these relations were only the germ of the lively commercial intercourse that
began to develop in the eleventh century, to be interrupted only
for a short time in the first period of the Crusades. After the
barrier of former ages had broken down, trade itself subsequently
became one of the strongest factors in promoting the transmission
of cultural values to the European peoples, who, aided by their
rulers (as Roger of Sicily) were eagerly seeking to benefit by them.

The manifold ways in which commercial relations led to close
co-operation between Muslims and Christians—e.g. in the form
of joint partnerships and of commercial treaties—cannot be treated
here in detail. The great riches of material culture, which the
Islamic world had gathered for nearly five centuries, were poured
down upon Europe. These riches consisted not only of Chinese,
Indian, and African products, which the enterprising spirit of Islam
had fetched from far-distant lands; they were in the first place
represented by what the Muhammadan countries themselves yielded
of natural and industrial products. Industrial production in
Muhammadan countries had developed in a particular way; it was
chiefly characterized by being completely under the control of the
rulers, by its lack of capital, and by its organization of the craftsmen
in guilds. This peculiar form of industrial development proved a
great disadvantage to Islam when it came, in later times, into
economic competition with European industry; but at the time of
Islamic prosperity it had made possible a development of industrial
skill which brought the artistic value of the products to an un-

equalled height. In the first place should be mentioned the products of the textile industry; a number of names, now commonly in use, shows which textiles were originally imported from Islamic countries: muslin (from Mosul), damask (from Damascus), balda-chin (originally a stuff made in Baghdād), and other woven stuffs, which bear Arabic or Persian names, like gauze, cotton, satin, &c. The import of oriental rugs is likewise as old as the Middle ages. It is curious to note, too, that the state robes of the medieval German Emperors bore Arabic inscriptions; they were ordered and executed probably in Sicily, where Islamic art and industry continued for a long time after the Christian reconquest. Natural products, which, by their name, betray their original importation from Muham-madan countries, are fruits like the orange, lemon, and apricot, vegetables such as spinach and artichokes, further saffron, and the now so important aniline. Likewise names of precious stones (lapis lazuli) and of musical instruments (lute, guitar, &c.), though it can-not be proved that the borrowing of these terms goes back directly to commercial intercourse. The same is to be said about so im-portant a material as paper, the fabrication of which Europe learnt from the Muhammadan peoples in the twelfth century.

Finally, our commercial vocabulary itself has preserved some very eloquent proofs of the fact that there was a time when Islamic trade and trade customs exercised a deep influence on the commercial development in Christian countries. In the word "sterling", for example, is contained the ancient Greek word "stater," but it has reached the English language only through the medium of Arabic. The word "traffic" itself probably is to be derived from the Arabic *tafrīq*, which means distribution, and such a well-known word as "tariff" is nothing but the good Arabic *ta'rīf*, meaning announce-ment. To the same origin belong the words "risk," "tare," "calibre," and the everyday word "magazine," from Arabic *makhāzin*, meaning stores (the French "magasin" is still the common word for shop). The "cheque" has already been mentioned in the description of the African trade, and the German and Dutch words for the same thing (*Wechsel, wissel*) are equally Arabic. So is also the term "aval." Next to the knowledge of the bill of exchange the con-ception of the joint-stock company was acquired by the partnership of Muslim and Christian Italian merchants. Muhammadan mercan-tile law was based only theoretically on the Sacred Law, derived from the Qurān and the sacred tradition; practically it was governed by a developed system of trade customs, to which the instances cited

above bear witness. One of these trade forms was also the feigned
bargain called "mohatra," which word had also passed from Arabic
into European languages.

A largely used word like "douane" is a reminder of the time when
regular commercial intercourse had developed in different ports of
the Mediterranean. It is well known that this intercourse has also
reacted largely on the commercial organization of western nations.
The treaties which they concluded with Muhammadan rulers, and
the institution of consular representatives in eastern ports, have
been important stages in the development of the rules that now-
adays govern international trade.

As may be seen from the previous observations, the cultural gain,
which Europe has acquired from the Islamic world in the domain
of geography and commerce, is not the fruit of one moment, but is
based on the mutual relations that have gone on since the beginning of the eleventh century and were especially lively during the
Mongol period in the thirteenth century. Also the fact that Islamic
civilization with its accretions has been continued by States such as
Turkey, Persia, and Muhammadan peoples in India and the East
Indies, has caused many Islamic views and customs to become
known and even practised in European countries. But no period
shows so clearly the once enormous superiority of the Islamic
peoples over the Christian world as the tenth century, when Islam
was at the summit of its prosperity and Christian Europe had come
to a seemingly hopeless standstill.

6 FROM   *Charles H. Haskins*

THE RENAISSANCE OF THE TWELFTH CENTURY

The classic account of Arabic influence on the development of Western European philosophy and science during the High Middle Ages was written by Professor Haskins many years ago. Although our knowledge of this facet of medieval civilization is much greater than when Haskins wrote, and although many details have been added to our knowledge, the main picture remains as he presented it. What stands out is the fact that it was by way of Spain and Sicily rather than the Holy Land of the Crusading Kingdoms that superior Moslem culture reached the West, and that Jewish scholars played an outstanding role in the process. The thoughtful reader will also note that learning only went one way, and that the Moslem world did not gain from the West any intellectual stimulus to match that which it exported to an interested Latin Christendom.

Until the twelfth century the intellectual contacts between Christian Europe and the Arab world were few and unimportant. They belong almost entirely to the age of the Crusades, but they owe very little to the Crusades themselves. The Crusaders were men of action, not men of learning, and little can be traced in the way of translations in Palestine and Syria. The known translators in Syria, Stephen of Pisa, *ca.* 1127, and Philip of Tripoli a century later, are little more than names to us, the former associated with the medicine of Ali-ben-Abbas, the latter with that widely popular work, *The Secret of Secrets*, which passed under the name of Aristotle. Adelard of Bath also visited Syria early in the twelfth century, but we do not know that he carried any texts away with him. North Africa had been Mohammedan since the seventh century, and although it boasted comparatively few schools of its own, it was the great highway between the East and Spain. Thither in course of time came certain adventurous Italians like Constantine the African—Italian at least by adoption, for he died a monk of Monte Cassino—and Leonard of Pisa. Constantine seems to have given a new impulse to

SOURCE. Charles H. Haskins, *The Renaissance of the Twelfth Century* (Cambridge, Mass.: Harvard University Press. Copyright, 1927, by the President and Fellows of Harvard College; 1955, by Clare Allen Haskins), pp. 282–291, 310–314. Reprinted by permission of the publisher.

medicine by his translations of Galen and Hippocrates and Isaac
the Jew, while Leonard of Pisa, son of a Pisan Customs official in
North Africa, acquired there a familiarity with Arabic mathematics
which made him the leading European mathematician of the thirteenth century. There was one Italian land which took more direct
part in the movement, namely Sicily. Midway between Europe and
Africa, Sicily had been under Arab rule from 902 to 1091, and under
the Normans who followed it retained a large Mohammedan element in its population. Moreover, it had many commercial relations
with Mohammedan countries, while King Roger conducted campaigns in Northern Africa and Frederick II made an expedition to
Palestine. Arabian physicians and astrologers were employed at the
Sicilian court, and one of the great works of Arabic learning, the
Geography of Edrisi, was composed at King Roger's command. A
contemporary scholar, Eugene the Emir, translated the *Optics* of
Ptolemy, while under Frederick II Michael Scot and Theodore of
Antioch made versions of Arabic works on zoölogy for the Emperor's use. Frederick also maintained a correspondence on
scientific topics with many sovereigns and scholars of Mohammedan
lands, and the work of translation went on under his son and successor Manfred, while we should probably refer to this Sicilian
centre some of the versions by unknown authors.

Nevertheless the most important channel by which the new learning reached Western Europe ran through the Spanish peninsula. . . .
In consequence of the Saracen conquest, the Peninsula became for
the greater portion of the Middle Ages a part of the Mohammedan East, heir to its learning and its science, to its magic and
astrology, and the principal means of their introduction into
Western Europe. When, in the twelfth century, the Latin world
began to absorb this Oriental lore, the pioneers of the new learning
turned chiefly to Spain, where one after another sought the key to
knowledge in the mathematics and astronomy, the astrology and
medicine and philosophy which were there stored up; and throughout the twelfth and thirteenth centuries Spain remained the land of
mystery, of the unknown yet knowable, for inquiring minds beyond
the Pyrenees. The great adventure of the European scholar lay in
the Peninsula.

In general, the lure of Spain began to act only in the twelfth
century, and the active impulse toward the spread of Arabic learning came from beyond the Pyrenees and from men of diverse
origins. The chief names are Adelard of Bath, Plato of Tivoli,

Robert of Chester, Hermann of Carinthia, with his pupil Rudolf of Bruges, and Gerard of Cremona, while in Spain itself we have Dominicus Gondisalvi, Hugh of Santalla, and a group of Jewish scholars, Petrus Alphonsi, John of Seville, Savasorda, and Abraham ben Ezra. Much in their biography and relations with one another is still obscure. Their work was at first confined to no single place, but translation was carried on at Barcelona, Tarazona, Segovia, Leon, Pamplona, as well as beyond the Pyrenees at Toulouse, Béziers, Narbonne, and Marseilles. Later, however, the chief centre became Toledo. An exact date for this new movement cannot be fixed, now that criticism has removed the year 1116 from an early title of Plato of Tivoli, but the astronomical tables of Adelard are dated 1126, and this whole group of translators, save Gerard of Cremona, can be placed within the second quarter of the twelfth century. They owed much to ecclesiastical patronage, especially to Raymond, archbishop of Toledo, and his contemporary Michael, bishop of Tarazona. Besides a large amount of astrology, inevitable in an age which regarded astrology as merely applied astronomy and a study of great practical utility, their attention was given mainly to astronomy and mathematics.

The latter half of the twelfth century saw the most industrious and prolific of all these translators from the Arabic, Gerard of Cremona. Fortunately we have a brief biographical note and list of his works, drawn up by his pupils in imitation of the catalogue of Galen's writings and affixed to Gerard's version of Galen's *Tegni*, lest the translator's light be hidden under a bushel and others receive credit for work which he left anonymous. From this we learn that, a scholar from his youth and master of the content of Latin learning, he was drawn to Toledo by love of Ptolemy's *Almagest*, which he could not find among the Latins. There he discovered a multitude of Arabic books in every field, and, pitying the poverty of the Latins, learned Arabic in order to translate them. His version of the *Almagest* bears the date of 1175. Before his death, which came at Toledo in 1187 at the age of seventy-three, he had turned into Latin the seventy-one Arabic works of this catalogue, besides perhaps a score of others. Three of these are logical, the *Posterior Analytics* of Aristotle with the commentaries of Themistius and al-Farabi; several are mathematical, including Euclid's *Elements*, the *Spherics* of Theodosius, a tract of Archimedes, and various treatises on geometry, algebra, and optics. The catalogue of works on astronomy and astrology is considerable, as is also the list of the scientific writings of Aristotle, but the longest list of all is medical, Galen and Hippocrates and the rest, who were chiefly known in these versions throughout the later Middle Ages. Indeed, more of Arabic science in general passed into Western Europe at the hands of Gerard of Cremona than in any other way.

After Gerard of Cremona, Roger Bacon lists Alfred the Englishman, Michael Scot, and Hermann the German as the principal translators from the Arabic, all of whom worked in Spain in the earlier thirteenth century. Alfred was a philosopher, concerned especially with expounding the natural philosophy of Aristotle, although he was also known for his version of two pseudo-Aristotelian treatises. Michael Scot first appears at Toledo in 1217 as the translator of al-Bitrogi *On the Sphere*, and by 1220 he had made the standard Latin version of Aristotle *On Animals*, not to mention his share in the transmission of the commentaries of Averroës on Aristotle and his own important works on astrology. Hermann the German, toward the middle of the century, was likewise concerned with Aristotle and Averroës, particularly the *Ethics*, *Poetics*, and *Rhetoric* and the commentaries thereon. Lesser writers of the same period concerned themselves with astrology and medicine.

None of these men from beyond the Pyrenees seems to have known Arabic when he came to Spain, some not when they left, and they worked perforce through interpreters, usually converted Jews. Thus while Gerard of Cremona used a Mozarab named Galippus, Michael Scot is said to have owed much to a Jew named Andrew, who is probably identical with Master Andrew, canon of Palencia, whom the Pope praises in 1225 for his knowledge of Arabic, Hebrew, Chaldee, and Latin, as well as the seven liberal arts. Sometimes Jews are themselves the authors or translators, as in the case of Petrus Alphonsi, John of Seville, Abraham ibn Ezra, and the astronomers of Alfonso X. Apparently their interpreting frequently took the form of translating from Arabic into the current Spanish idiom, which the Christian translator then turned into Latin. This fact helps to explain the inaccuracies of many of the versions, although in general they are slavishly literal, even to carrying over the Arabic article. We must also bear in mind that there was a large amount of translation from Arabic into Hebrew and then later into Latin, as any one can verify by turning to Steinschneider's great volume on Hebrew translations.

In this process of translation and transmission accident and convenience played a large part. No general survey of the material was made, and the early translators groped somewhat blindly in the mass of new matter suddenly disclosed to them. Brief works were often taken first because they were brief and the fundamental treatises were long and difficult; commentators were often preferred to the subject of the commentary. Moreover, the translators worked in different places, so that they might easily duplicate one another's work, and the earliest or more accurate version was not always the most popular. Much was translated to which the modern world is indifferent, something was lost which we should willingly recover, yet the sum total is highly significant. From Spain came the philosophy and natural science of Aristotle and his Arabic commentators in the form which was to transform European thought in the thirteenth century. The Spanish translators made most of the current versions of Galen and Hippocrates and of the Arab physicians like Avicenna. Out of Spain came the new Euclid, the new algebra, and treatises on perspective and optics. Spain was the home of astronomical tables and astronomical observation from the days of Maslama and al-Zarkali to those of Alfonso the Wise, and the meridian of Toledo was long the standard of computation for the West, while we must also note the current compends of astronomy, like al-Fargani, as well as the generally received version of Ptolemy's *Almagest*, for the love of which Gerard of Cremona made the long journey to Toledo. The great body of Eastern astrology came through Spain, as did something of Eastern alchemy.

This Spanish tide flowed over the Pyrenees into Southern France, to centres like Narbonne, Béziers, Toulouse, Montpellier, and Marseilles, where the new astronomy appears as early as 1139 and traces can also be found of the astrology, philosophy, and medicine of the Arabs on into the fourteenth century. Here the share of Jewish translators was large, perhaps even larger relatively than in Spain; and many of the versions came by way of the Hebrew.

Besides these known works in the several Mediterranean lands, a place must also be kept for the numerous translations from the Arabic of which both author and land are unknown. Here we must group, not only much scattered material of minor importance, especially in astrology, but also certain fundamental works like the *Physics, Metaphysics*, and several lesser works of Aristotle on natural science, as these appear in the West about 1200. There is also at least one anonymous version from the Arabic of the *Almagest* and the *Quadripartitum* of Ptolemy. With minor exceptions no names of translators are attached to the Latin literature of alchemy which

purports to come from the Arabic, like the writings of the so-called
Geber.

The indebtedness of the Western world to the Arabs is well
illustrated in the scientific and commercial terms which its various
languages have borrowed untranslated from the Arabic. Words like
algebra, zero, cipher tell their own tale, as do "Arabic" numerals
and the word algorism which long distinguished their use as taught
by al-Khwarizmi. In astronomy the same process is exemplified in
almanac, zenith, nadir, and azimuth. From the Arabic we get
alchemy, and perhaps chemistry, as well as alcohol, alkali, elixir,
alembic, not to mention pharmaceutical terms like syrup and gum
arabic. In the field of trade and navigation we have bazar and tariff,
admiral and arsenal, and products of Mohammedan lands such as
sugar and cotton, the muslin of Mosul and the damask of Damascus,
the leather of Cordova and Morocco. Such fossils of our vocabulary reveal whole chapters of human intercourse in the
Mediterranean.

· · · · ·

Let us turn now to science. We shall get a better measure of the
progress made in the twelfth century by surveying rapidly the several
fields of science. Let us begin with mathematics. In the scheme of
mediaeval education comprised in the seven liberal arts, four of
these, or the *quadrivium*, were considered mathematical, namely,
arithmetic, geometry, astronomy, and music; but their mathematics
was very elementary indeed. How elementary, appears not only
from the textbooks of Boethius and Bede, with their very simple
outlines of arithmetical and astronomical reckoning, but also from
the extraordinary reputation which Gerbert acquired when he went
somewhat beyond these masters. Confined to the material contained in Boethius and in fragments of the Roman *agrimensores*,
Gerbert seems to have revived the practical use of the abacus, or
counting-table of the Romans, which had a great vogue in the
eleventh and twelfth centuries. Though he gave certain mysterious
names and symbols to its counters, he did not use the Arabic
method of reckoning by position, and devotes tedious chapters to a
description of the "iron process" of long division with Roman
numerals. In geometry he knew only the most elementary parts of
Euclid; in astronomy, in spite of the wonder which his simple
apparatus excited, he does not seem to have gone beyond Bede. The
mathematical labors of the following century in Lorraine and at

Chartres were devoted to keeping alive the Gerbertian tradition. Nevertheless, the number of manuscripts *ca*, 1100 which deal with the elements of arithmetical and astronomical computation is a clear indication of the intellectual revival.

Early in the twelfth century the whole of Euclid's *Elements* of geometry appeared in a Latin translation, apparently from the Arabic, and a generation later his *Data* and *Optics* were accessible to more advanced students. Geometry had reached substantially the position which it occupied until recent times. In 1126 Adelard of Bath brought the trigonometrical tables of al-Khwarizmi to the West. In 1145 Robert of Chester translated the *Algebra* of the same author into Latin, thus introducing the name as well as the processes of this science into Christian Europe. This book "on the restoration and opposition of numbers" (*Liber algebre et almucabola*) "laid the foundations of modern analysis," as the curious reader may see from Professor Karpinski's English translation, where the equations are given in modern notation. Al-Khwarizmi's name, softened into "algorismus" and finally in Chaucer into "augrim," became attached to the new Indian arithmetic, of which the first Latin version meets us about the same time. Arabic numerals came in the course of the century, very possibly transmitted through the operations of trade rather than in academic manuals; but by the end of the century the learned world is divided between the algorists, who upheld the new method of reckoning, and the older abacists, who secured legislation against the use of the new-fangled figures at Florence as late as 1299. In 1202 appeared the earliest book of Leonard of Pisa, the *Liber abaci*, followed by the epoch-making treatises in which this mathematical genius gave solutions of quadratic and cubic equations and otherwise showed his "sovereign possession of the mathematical knowledge of his own and every preceding generation." Algebra had now reached a point from which it was not to make notable advances until the sixteenth century. The decisive importance of the twelfth century is nowhere more evident.

The astronomical manuscripts of the beginning of the century consist mainly of copies or extracts from the manuals of Bede and the Carolingian computist Helperic, with some attention to ecclesiastical chronology as touching the date of the Christian era. The few references which are found to the Arabic astrolabe do not indicate any further acquaintance with Arabic astronomy, so that the Anglo-Norman *Cumpoz* of Philippe de Thaon in 1119 reflects only the older Latin tradition. In the following year, however, another Englishman, Walcher of Malvern, begins to reckon by degrees, minutes, and seconds, as he has learned them from a Spanish Jew named Petrus Alphonsi, and in 1126 Adelard of Bath translates the astronomical tables of al-Khwarizmi. These were soon followed by the tables of al-Battani and al-Zarkali and by the brief manual of al-Fargani. Ptolemy's famous *Almagest*, that comprehensive summary of ancient astronomy, was translated from the Greek about 1160 and from the Arabic in 1175. Henceforth the full reception of the astronomical knowledge of the ancient world depended upon the assimilation of this work.

Meanwhile the Aristotelian physics had begun to filter in through Arabic writers, and the conflict of this with Ptolemy, as well as with Plato's *Timaeus*, puzzled an age which desired at all costs to reconcile its standard authorities. Aristotle's *Physics* was translated not long before 1200, but his *Meteorology* had been accessible before 1162 and the *De caelo* perhaps as early, while fragments of Aristotle's physical doctrines came in through various channels in the course of the century. As we approach 1200, we find an increasing number of brief treatises which discuss the nature of the universe and its elements and the phenomena of earthquakes and tides and volcanoes. The meteorology of the age is definitely Aristotelian.

Its geography, strangely enough, remains essentially Roman, limited for the most part to Ptolemy and Isidore. There was, we have seen, a widening of Europe's geographical horizon by the crusading expeditions and by explorations to the North and Northeast, with a corresponding expansion of the sphere of European civilization, but there was no accompanying reception of Arabic geography. "The works of the foremost Mohammedan geographers, Al-Mas'udi, Ibn Hauqal, Al-Istakhri, were unknown in Europe during the Middle Ages, and formal Arabic geography certainly contributed next to nothing to the knowledge of the earth possessed by the Occidentals of the Crusading age."

PART THREE

Alienation and Divergence—from the End of the Crusading States in Syria to the Fall of Granada, A.D. 1291–1492

During the two centuries of the Later Middle Ages, the hostility which had already arisen between the Islamic world and the Latin West continued and deepened. More important, the institutions and ideals of these two contiguous civilizations diverged almost totally. This divergence is most noticeable when one compares the political progress of France, England, Spain, and Italy, for example, with the slave state system prevailing in Mamluke Egypt or the Sultanate of Delhi; or when one contrasts the intellectual ferment in Western Christian university circles with the intellectual torpor in the growing Empire of the Ottoman Turks, the ephemeral realm of Tamurlane, or the small states of Moslem North Africa. The Islamic world continued to prize a mystical vision in religion, a glorious art and architecture, and a rather flowery traditional poetic literature, but it no longer valued the philosophical and scientific investigations that now flourished in the West.

Perhaps it is this hostility and divergence which explain the cool, detached, critical way in which Ibn Khaldûn presents his view of the Christian Church (Selection 2). Yet Christian–Moslem divergence was never total. Advances in military technology were instantly copied in both civilizations, and trade between the two remained brisk. It flourished along Mediterranean and Black Sea routes which continued to be dominated by the fleets of Genoese, Venetian, and Catalan merchants. These Western traders exchanged the ship timber, war materials, and slaves which Moslem rulers needed to defend themselves, for the silks and spices of the

Far East to which Western Europe had become accustomed. Even pilgrimage to the Holy Land continued uninterrupted after its reconquest by Mamluke Sultans.

Yet it needs to be emphasized that such contacts were carried on despite outbreaks of militancy on both sides. The Latin West maintained a continuous crusading spirit, and the Islamic East a perpetual *jihad* or Holy War (Selection 1). This was particularly true when the Ottoman Turks began to spread their dominion from Asia Minor into the heart of the Balkans (Selection 3), provoking a spasmodic and unsuccessful series of reactions from the Christian West. Eventually, by 1453, this conflict resulted in the Fall of Constantinople and the appearance of a hostile Ottoman Empire in the Balkans and the Mediterranean (Selection 4), which was long to threaten the military security of Western Europe itself.

Ultimately the Turkish menace inspired a revived crusading spirit in both the Eastern Mediterranean and the Iberian peninsula. This spirit, increasingly linked to a new commercial vision, inspired Prince Henry the Navigator to send his ships down the West Coast of Africa (Selection 5) and induced Ferdinand and Isabella to conquer Granada (Selection 6). It drove Columbus westward to reach American shores, and it prompted the Portuguese to round the Cape of Good Hope and establish a sea route to India. In all these ventures the Spanish and Portuguese people were filled with an anti-Islamic militancy that was to color Western European contacts with the Moslem world in the centuries to come.

1 FROM *Aziz S. Atiya*

THE LATER CRUSADES

This general introduction to the later crusades in the Eastern Mediterranean emphasizes that the end of the Middle Ages saw no basic change in the crusading idea. Throughout the fourteenth and fifteenth centuries, crusades continued to be launched and crusading propaganda remained widespread throughout the Latin West, even though little was achieved in the way of permanent success. Atiya's explanation for this, especially with regard to the military skill of Egypt's Mamlukes, deserves particular attention. On the other hand, recent historical research suggests that Atiya has overestimated the prosperity of Mamluke Egypt. The failure of the late medieval Crusades resulted not from the strength of Islam but rather from Europe's weakness and concern with other matters.

It might appear from the multiplicity of the signs of change that in the Later Middle Ages the crusade became a moribund ideal beyond human power to resuscitate. This opinion, indeed, has been held by a series of distinguished historians, and the view is still expressed that the expulsion of the Latins from the Holy Land in the last decade of the thirteenth century marked the end of the holy war. It must now, however, be recognized that the crusade and the crusading impulse outlived the Kingdom of Jerusalem as it had existed on the Asiatic mainland for at least two centuries, during which projects for Eastern expeditions remained one of the vital forces in European politics notwithstanding all the adverse circumstances already enumerated. This is the sum-total of the thesis

SOURCE. Aziz Suryal Atiya, *The Crusade in the Later Middle Ages* (London: Methuen & Co., Ltd., 1938), pp. 10–25. Reprinted by permission of the publisher.

underlying the whole of this present account, and at this juncture
we must indicate certain of the forces which kept the crusade alive
in the minds of the statesmen, churchmen, and "common" people
of the age.

Events in the Levant during the fourteenth and fifteenth centuries
were moving with much rapidity and in such a direction as to keep
the West aware of the growing Saracen menace to the few remaining
Christian outposts in those regions. Moreover, the calamities
threatening the Catholic nations in east central Europe at the hand
of the Ottoman Turk, had a most disquieting influence on the rest
of Christendom. The fall of 'Akka in 1291, although long foreseen,
caused great alarm and indignation in Europe. The complete con-
solidation of Syria under Muslim rule for the first time since the
beginning of the crusades at the end of the eleventh century appears
to have fostered the spirit of aggression among the Mamlūk Sultans
of Egypt and their Amīrs, who pursued their career of conquest
further north into the Christian Kingdom of Lesser Armenia. Owing
to her proximity to the empire of the Egyptians in northern Syria,
Armenia became their next objective and its forts were destroyed
one by one, its prosperous towns pillaged and its fields laid waste.
The Armenian people represented the latest triumph of Catholicism
in the East. In the early years of the fourteenth century, their kingdom was one on the edge of ruin; and, to save it from utter extinction, they renounced their old creed, submitted to the authority of
Rome, and appealed to the West for succour. Leaving on one side
the controversial subject of the genuineness of the Armenian conversion, we may say that a moral duty fell upon Western Europe
to protect and preserve from destruction this much-oppressed
kingdom. In spite of this, Armenia was finally annexed by the Amīr
of Halab (Aleppo) in 1375 and King Leo VI was captured and
carried to the Citadel of Cairo where he remained in chains until
1382. This disaster aroused great indignation in Europe and stirred
up the enthusiasm of western people for the crusade. The fate
of the little Latin Kingdom of Cyprus under the House of Lusignan
was not very much better than the lot of her Armenian sister on the
mainland. Although protected by the waters of the Mediterranean,
she survived her by only a few decades. As soon as the Egyptians
were able to equip a fleet and launch it against Cyprus, the fate of
the island was sealed. Three naval expeditions in 1424, 1425 and
1426 brought pillage and destruction on the kingdom and ended in
the capture of King Janus, who, like Leo the Armenian, was carried

in chains to Cairo. He was released only after the payment of a
heavy ransom, and after swearing allegiance to Sultan Bursbai and
promising to pay him an annual tribute. The Egyptian chroniclers
concur in telling us that Janus recovered his freedom after becoming one of the Sultan's Mamlūks and his viceroy in the kingdom
that had been his own. What effect these successive disasters had in
the West, remains to be seen in the following pages. The turn of
Rhodes, too, was soon to follow in the expeditions of 1440, 1443,
and 1445. Although Egypt fared ill in its attempts to overthrow the
Knights of St. John, the Egyptian wars formed a precedent for
Muslim attacks on the island fortress and prepared the way for the
final expulsion of the Order from Cyprus at a later stage by the
Ottomans in the reign of Sultan Suleiman the Magnificent. While
these conflicts were bringing to a speedy and tragic end the in-
efficient rule of Latin Christianity in the East, the Ottomans had
been marching with bewildering rapidity towards the heart of
Catholic Christendom in Europe. The defeat of the united forces of
the West outside the city of Nicopolis in 1396 and the final destruction of the shadow of the ancient empire of Constantinople in
1453 had ensured the hold of the Turks over the Balkans and
enabled their armies to follow the road of invasion to Buda and to
Vienna. As early as the reign of Murad I (1359–89), the Sultan,
according to French pilgrims, had sworn to "come to France when
he had finished with Austria" and had also pledged himself to ride
to Rome and turn the altar of St. Peter's into a manger for his
horse. Even if Europe was not in the mood to make any further
attempts to subdue the East and save the Holy Land from the
unbeliever, it seemed as though a crusade would be needed to save
Eastern and Central Europe from the Turkish menace.

The Papacy, despite its trials and tribulation during the periods
of the Babylonish Captivity, the Great Schism and the distracting
influence of the Conciliar Movement, never lost sight of the
Crusade. The earnest attempt of the papal curia to convert the
Tartars to Catholicism and so secure their help and support for an
effective crusade is only one demonstration of the activity of the
Church. To say that the Avignonese papacy had become subject to
the will of the kings of France and that it had completely neglected
its duties, in which the crusade remained a vital element, would be
both misleading and unjust. Contemporary documents prove
beyond all doubt the weakness of such contentions, Clement V
(1305–14), the first of the Avignonese popes in the period of the

Babylonish Captivity, seems to have accumulated the large sum of 300,000 gold florins to be used for the cause of the crusade. When Clement died before the realization of his project, the money was left in the Château de Monteux in the diocese of Carpentras in the custody of his nephew, Bertrand de Got, vicomte de Lomagne, who retained the treasure, probably aiming to appropriate all or part of it to himself. John XXII, who succeeded to the papal chair, wished to recover this money and put it to its proper use according to the express will of his predecessor. Hence a protracted process was opened in the course of which several appeals were issued to the Kings of England and France to settle this and the more important matter of the crusade. Of the support given by Clement VI to King Hugh de Lusignan at the battle of Smyrna (1344) and to Humbert de Viennois in the crusade of 1345, by Innocent VI to Pierre I de Lusignan in his attack on Adalia (1361), by Urban V to the crusaders of Alexandria (1365) and to the enterprise of Amedeo VI of Savoy (1363–6), and by other popes and anti-popes to the Barbary expedition (1390) and the crusade of Nicopolis (1396), much will be said in these pages.

· · · · ·

In an age of faith, the idea of saving the Holy Places could not possibly sink into complete oblivion. No doubt, there were periods of indifference and forgetfulness towards a cause for which so much Christian blood had been shed in bygone centuries. Yet, reminders of the state of the Christians of the East and the duty incumbent upon their fellow-men in the West were numerous. Travellers came back from the Levant with tales of suffering, sacrilege and misery; but perhaps the most potent of reminders were the wandering princes of Christian Kingdoms, now extinct or on the verge of extinction at the hand of the Saracen. The first and perhaps the most moving of the cases was that of King Leo VI of Armenia, who, after having lost his country and his crown, and after having been incarcerated in Cairo for seven long years (1375–82), was at last released on the payment of his ransom by the Church and on condition that he should not return to his native land. The King went to and fro in the West, and after visiting the courts of both Urban VI and Clement VII, retired to Paris where he lived on charity until he died in November 1393 without leaving an heir to his lost kingdom. The Western journeys of Pierre I de Lusignan, 1362–5, too, served as another reminder of a totally different kind. Owing to the high place occupied by this "athleta Christi" in the fourteenth-century movement, his travels in Europe will be considered in detail at a later stage. In the fifteenth century the main emissaries of the East came from the crumbling Empire of Constantinople. After the crushing defeat of the Latins at Nicopolis in 1396, Manuel II Palaeologos was forced to swear allegiance to the Ottoman victor, Bayezid I. Seeing, however, that the downfall of his last stronghold in the forsaken city of Constantine was merely a matter of time, he departed on a "mendicant Pilgrimage" to the West, hoping against hope that he might rouse his fellow-Christians to come to his aid and save the miserable remnant of his Empire. He wandered from one court to another in Italy, France and England during the years 1399–1401. Benedict IX, the Roman Pope, responded by sending Paul, Bishop of Chalcedon, and Ilario Doria, Knight of Genoa, "to England and other parts" to preach the crusade against the Turks. The Duke of Milan gave Manuel some valuable presents, and Charles VI of France granted him a pension of 30,000 crowns. In England, he was met by Henry IV himself at Blackheath and taken to the royal palace at Eltham for Christmas. On his return, however, Manuel found that his beleaguered capital was saved for a time, thanks to Timur's victory over Bayezid I in the battle of Angora (28 July 1402) and not to the imperial intercession at the courts of Europe. After the fall of Constantinople and the flight of the last of the Palaeologos dynasty to the Morea, one of their number, Thomas Palaeologos, took refuge in Rome in 1461, bringing with him the head of St. Andrew the Apostle. His presence added to the anger of Pius II against the Turk and made him determined to fulfil his project of crusade at any cost. The sad fate of dwindling monarchies and the wanderings of august kings and emperors among the peoples of Western Europe could not but inflame the ardour of men and women among whom the crusade was still a living memory.

Last but not least was the great energy displayed in the writings of pilgrims and propagandists of the Later Middle Ages for the old cause. The enormous body of literature emanating from the pen of these enthusiasts is indeed one of the permanent monuments of the time and justifies the special attention which will be accorded to it in the following pages. If the crusade had aroused so much sympathy in Europe, how can we account for the meagreness of its outcome and the ultimate failure of the movement as a whole? The futility of all efforts to save the Holy Land might be ascribed in part to the circumstances of European politics already outlined in this chapter. On the other hand, the state of the Islamic world was yet another principal element in the frustration and collapse of the crusading movement. It would be idle to dwell on all the events and institutions which formed the basic strength of Egypt in Asia and of Turkey in Europe, although a brief survey of some of these seems both necessary and helpful.

Egypt in the fourteenth and fifteenth centuries was one of the most prosperous countries in the world. The description of Cairo and Alexandria by late medieval travellers, frequently quoted in the first part of this study, and the accounts of the contemporary Egyptian chroniclers, read like a fairy tale. . . .

The chief source of this fabulous wealth was not Egypt itself, whose arable land was limited to a comparatively small and narrow strip of soil on the banks of the Nile in times when the modern irrigation system was unknown. It was not only in articles of luxury that the natural resources of Egypt were defective, but also in some of the primary raw materials, necessary for the maintenance of a large army. Egypt had no forests to supply timber for the construction of fleets and no mines to furnish the Sultans with the raw metals for the manufacture of implements of war. The secret of the prosperity of the country was trade. Egypt, and for that matter Syria also, happened to be in possession of the nearest and most practical termini of the Eastern trade routes by the Red Sea and by the Euphrates and Persia to India. Other routes to Caffa, Trebizond and Armenia existed, but they did not rival the former in facility and cheapness; and, moreover, it must be remembered that the market-towns of Christian Armenia were closed by the Egyptians after that country had been seized by them in the course of the fourteenth century. The merchants of the West had no choice but to resort to the markets of Alexandria, Damascus and other important towns in the Mamlūk Empire for their trade requirements. The solidity and efficiency of an elaborate and centralized administrative system, without equal except perhaps in some of the Italian republics, ensured a regular and undiminished revenue for the Sultan's coffers. This money was not, at least wholly, spent on luxuries and amusements for the ruler in power. The major part of it was used for the maintenance of a standing army, sufficiently well-equipped and well-trained to stem the tide of invasion by the crusaders from Western Europe on the one side and by the Mongols from the heart of Asia on the other. This army was annually re-

inforced by a few thousand young Mamlūks purchased for the
Sultan and his generals partly by Muslim agents who imported their
goods by land, but chiefly by Christian merchants and especially
the Genoese who transported their acquisitions from all the markets of Caffa and the Balkans by sea. It was a lucrative trade, and
the Italian merchants unscrupulously defied all the papal bulls
prohibiting it on pain of excommunication.

It is unnecessary here to moralize on the baseness of such trans-
actions on the part of the Italians, offending as they did against the
law of God and the interests of their fellow-Christians, or to dwell
too long on the ruthless and unscrupulous character of that enormous medieval "foreign legion" of Mamlūks. Whatever the rights
and wrongs of the case, the fact remains that, with the passing of
centuries since their introduction into Egypt and their ultimate
ascension to power in the state, the Mamlūks had succeeded in
fashioning one of the most redoubtable systems of medieval warfare, whose efficiency was proven in the long succession of en-
counters with the crusaders of the East. The abundant contemporary
Arabic literature dealing with the Mamlūk art of war may indeed
form a worthy basis for a much-needed and independent work on
the subject. At present, however, it will be illuminating to indicate
briefly some of the outstanding characteristics of that system. The
victory of the Mamlūks in battle was not necessarily the outcome
of sheer valour. In this, the Western combatants were equal, if not
superior to them. It was a question of tactics which aimed at the
dislocation of the enemy phalanxes and the confusion of his lines.
The skill of the Mamlūk fighters in archery, and the type of horse
they used, helped considerably towards this end. Mamlūks were
trained from early youth, not only to become great swordsmen and
lancers, but also and in particular to achieve excellence in the use
of the bow and arrow; and constant drilling during the rest of their
lives increased their attainments in this sphere. Then the Mamlūk
horse, lean but swift in action, presented a marked contrast to the
heavy Western horse; and, again, the Mamlūk soldier was lightly
clad while his Western opponent was mailed in steel. Even if we
overlook the conditions of battle under a fierce Eastern sun, a
point which Philippe de Mézières, chancellor of the kingdom of
Cyprus, made clear in his *Songe du vieil pelerin'*, this contrast alone
is sufficient to explain the defeat of the Christians and give us
reason to marvel at whatever triumphs they may have achieved. The
mobility of the Mamlūk line of battle enabled them both to harass

their enemy on all sides and to adapt their own formation and
tactics to any unforeseen development without much difficulty. When
hard-pressed in sieges, too, they knew what the West did not know
till very recent times—the use of "poisonous gases." Missiles and
Greek fire served their purpose well as long as the walls of a beleaguered city remained intact. On the other hand, a gap in the
wall or the boring of a mine—a favourite practice in European
warfare—would lead to a precarious battle at close quarters and
the uncertainty of hand-to-hand fighting with a steel-clad enemy.
To stop the onrush of besiegers into their stronghold, the Mamlūks
hit on the ingenious idea of baking inflammable discs capable of
emitting thick fumes of sulphur and ammonia. These were placed
in the defective parts of walls and in mines and set alight. Even if
such gases were not strictly poisonous according to the standards of
modern civilization, they were sufficiently pungent and obnoxious
to deter and demoralize the mailed knight in his slow movement.

On the religious side, it is extremely doubtful whether the
Mamlūks viewed the principle of holy war (al-Jihād) in the same
light and with the same earnestness as the apostles of primitive
Islam. Composed of Christian renegades who had betrayed their
God and renounced their faith, or recruited from distant regions
and tribes of obscure origin, they often gave themselves up to
excesses, debauchery and orgies of the worst type. Yet in public
they affected such a holy appearance and manner as to silence their
critics. On the other hand, the spirit of al-Jihād was consonant with
their warlike instincts, and this word was therefore continually used
to intensify the enthusiasm of all Muslims in their contests with
the crusaders. One very important feature of the Arabic literature
on the art of war was the form in which it was presented as advice
for holy warriors. The Mamlūk soldier, however ungodly he might
have been in the past, became a holy warrior in his contest with the
Christians; and when he fell in battle, he became a holy martyr.

The Ottoman Turks had much in common with the Mamlūks,
at least in regard to the matter of warfare. Their tactics were
similar, their horse was identical, and their attention to the art of
using the bow and arrow was equal. They also had their "foreign
legion," but on a much smaller scale, in the Janissaries, although
some writers are apt to antedate the importance of this future *corps
d'élite*. Their war, too, was a holy war (Jihād) with a somewhat
more genuine feeling about it than in the case of the Mamlūks. It
is also noteworthy that, whereas the Mamlūk Sultanate, like the

Holy Roman Empire in the West, was purely elective in principle—and hence suffered from the unending quarrels and many crimes caused by disputes over succession—the Ottomans had an established dynasty with fixed hereditary rights; and one of the happy features of its early history was the unbroken chain of strong monarchs who laid the foundation of a vast empire. On the other hand, it would be an error to magnify the power of the Ottomans beyond its definite limitations in the fourteenth century. Their European conquests were in great part made easy by the impotence of the countries which succumbed to their yoke. Further, the Ottomans were only one of many independent Turkish dynasties in Asia Minor, and far from being the strongest or wealthiest of them. It was not until the fifteenth century that the process of Turkish unification in Anatolia by means of a series of marriages, intrigues and conquests was complete. The Timurid invasion of the peninsula in 1402 either suppressed or at least reduced to impotence all the independent Turkish principalities and with them the remaining Christian fortresses on the Asiatic mainland. Bayezid I sustained the most humiliating defeat of his career and became Timur's prisoner for the rest of his life at Angora, but the Ottoman realm was intact beyond the Hellespont—a fact which may account in part for Ottoman recovery and supremacy over sister states in Asia. If the Crusade of Nicopolis (1396), either by accident or by design, had been postponed for six years until the time of the battle of Angora (1402), the power of the Ottomans might have been wrecked for ever, their rule in Europe nipped in the bud, and—who knows?—the dream of uniting the forces of the West and of the Far East in conjunction with Timur and Tatar against the Mamlūks realized and the Holy Land regained for Latin Christianity.

In the Balkans, the conditions that heralded the greatness of the Ottomans were of a different nature from those affecting Asia Minor. Their origin may be traced to the year 1345 when the usurper Kantakuzenos invited a detachment of Orkhan's army to cross the strait and assist him in his civil war with the child-emperor John V Palaeologos and the Dowager-Empress his mother. In return for this service against his own fellow-countrymen, Kantakuzenos undertook to marry his daughter Theodora to the Sultan and to allow his men to carry into slavery whomsoever they captured among the reluctant Greek followers of the legitimate emperor. This was the beginning of the end of the ancient empire. The Ottomans never retired from Thrace and they unremittingly pursued their

triumphant career after the deposition of Kantakuzenos. The field
was too rich and the booty too tempting to be given up without a
struggle. This struggle proved to be beyond the power of the
imperial host to sustain. Byzantium had fared ill at the hands of the
Latins in the Fourth Crusade in 1204. When the Latin Empire of
Constantinople was recovered by the Palaeologi in 1261, it was a
weak and divided land, composed of several petty fiefs under Latin
and Slavonic lords organized on an alien feudal model. The old
imperial theocracy was but a shadow of the past and the country
had become the prey of conflicting institutions, interests, races and
creeds. The hatred of the native Greeks for their arrogant foreign
masters was aggravated by the planting of Latin Catholicism in
their country. This absence of political independence and, what
meant even more to the Greek, the great menace to Eastern
Orthodoxy, changed the whole outlook of the inhabitants of the
Empire towards the Ottoman invasion. The advent of the Turk in
their midst was not considered as calamitous as it has often been
painted; for the new invader, though replacing the Latins in their
lordship of the land, promised to be more tolerant in religious
matters. The Greeks would willingly forfeit that slender hope of
political independence, if only they could save their church from
ruin. The Ottomans appeared in the Balkans at this juncture and
made use of these circumstances to establish their sway on European
soil. This baffling situation has its analogy in earlier Byzantine
history, when the "Jacobites" of Egypt treated with 'Amr ibn al-'Āṣ
and accepted the Covenant of Caliph 'Umar to save their Church
and country from the ruthless government of the Melkite Christians
in the days of Heraclius. Although the analogy is not altogether a
perfect one, in each case the surrender of liberties to an invading
race with a totally different religion was regarded as the lesser of
two evils.

The idea of the crusade in later medieval times was not confined
to Europe and the Levant. It was hoped that a third party—the
Tatar—would enter the field against the Muslims. In order to esti-
mate the extent and limitation of Mongol collaboration in holy
war, it may be helpful to outline the main features of the Mongol
state in the period under review. During the fourteenth century
their empire consisted of four distinct divisions—first, the Kipchak
realm in the steppes of south Russia; second, Persia whose government was disputed by a multitude of dynasties until Timur put an
end to all of them; third, the Chaghatai Empire, named after its

founder, a son of Chingiz Khan who held the greater part of Central
Asia; and fourth, the Far East under the dynasty of Qublay Khan.
At the close of the thirteenth century, the Mongols were still largely
pagan, and this gave rise to the great contest between the Christian
missionary and the Muslim traveller and merchant, each trying
desperately to win them for his faith, and the struggle ended in the
complete triumph of the latter. For the purposes of missionary
activity, the Roman Church created three large Oriental Sees—first,
the "Vicaria Tartariae Aquilonaris," comprising the Custodia
Gazariae (Khazars) on the north-western shores of the Black Sea
as well as the Sea of Azof and the "Custodia Sarai" between the
Black Sea and the Caspian; second, the "Vicaria Tartariae
Orientalis," comprising the "Custodia Trapezundis" (Trebizond)
and the "Custodia Thauris" (Tabrīz) which extended over Greater
Armenia, Mesopotamia and Persia with the town of Soldaia as the
seat of the Archbishop of Sultanieh; third, the "Vicaria Tartariae
seu Kathay," with Cambalec (the Arabic Khān Bāliq and the modern
Peking) as the seat of its archbishop until the expulsion of the
Mongols from China about the middle of the century. The con-
tiguity of Mongol dominion to the Holy Land together with the
great hatred of Tatar emperors for the Mamluk sultans encouraged
the Latins in their effort to bring this new race within the fold of
Catholicism and ultimately save the Holy Land with their aid. The
failure of this movement was not entirely due to the Mongol adoption of Islam as their state religion, but, rather to the inability of
the crusading countries to take united action at the right moment.
The death of Timur on 19 January 1405 precipitated the dismemberment of his vast empire and the final downfall of Mongol power
and influence in the Near East. Thus all hopes of a Romano-Tatar
crusade to crush Egypt and save the Holy Places were extinguished
in the course of the fifteenth century.

In the meantime, other great movements had shaken the very
foundation of the medieval world. The revival of classical scholarship had changed the old conception of life and learning, and the
age of discoveries opened up new fields for expansion and furnished
Europe with new bones of contention. The interests of the West
became more oceanic than Levantine, and the zeal for the crusade
was on the wane. Egypt, hitherto head of the Islamic world, succumbed to the conquering arm of the Turk (1517) and sank into the
obscurity of one of the darkest ages in all her history, while the
dawn of Modern History broke over Europe with the Renaissance.

2 TRANSLATED BY *Franz Rosenthal*

IBN KHALDÛN'S REMARKS ON JUDAISM AND CHRISTIANITY

In this passage Ibn Khaldûn, wisest of all Islamic social philosophers, discusses the history of the Jews and Christians. Although he makes some minor errors such as having Nebuchadnezzar destroy both the Kingdoms of Israel and Judah, or having the original Gospels of the New Testament written in Latin, his account seems remarkably close to the facts. On the other hand, he shows a basic lack of concern with the subtleties of Christian doctrine that distinguish Christian sects, and a lack of interest in monasticism in general. His view of both faiths, and especially Christianity, is a detached one, which accurately mirrors the lack of interest on the part of the average intellectual Moslem during the fourteenth and fifteenth centuries.

It should be known that after the removal of its prophet, a religious group must have someone to take care of it. (Such a person) must cause the people to act according to the religious laws. In a way, he stands to them in the place (*khalîfah*, caliph) of their prophet, in as much as (he urges) the obligations which (the prophet) had imposed upon them. Furthermore, in accordance with the afore-mentioned need to political leadership in social organization, the human species must have a person who will cause them to act in accordance with what is good for them and who will prevent them by force from doing things harmful to them. Such a person is the one who is called ruler.

In the Muslim community, the holy war is a religious duty, because of the universalism of the (Muslim) mission and (the obligation to) convert everybody to Islam either by persuasion or by force. Therefore, caliphate and royal authority are united in (Islam), so that the person in charge can devote the available strength to both of them at the same time.

The other religious groups did not have a universal mission, and the holy war was not a religious duty to them, save only for purposes of defense. It has thus come about that the person in charge

SOURCE. Ibn Khaldûn, *The Muqaddimah*, trans. by Franz Rosenthal, Bollingen Series XLIII (New York: Princeton University Press; London: Routledge & Kegan Paul Ltd. Copyright, 1958, by Bollingen Foundation), Vol. I, pp. 472–481. Reprinted by permission.

of religious affairs (other religious groups) is not concerned with power politics at all. (Among them,) royal authority comes to those who have it, by accident and in some way that has nothing to do with religion. It comes to them as the necessary result of group feeling, which by its very nature seeks to obtain royal authority, as we have mentioned before, and not because they are under obligation to gain power over other nations, as is the case with Islam. They are merely required to establish their religion among their own (people).

This is why the Israelites after Moses and Joshua remained unconcerned with royal authority for about four hundred years. Their only concern was to establish their religion.

· · · · ·

The Israelites dispossessed the Canaanites of the land that God had given them as their heritage in Jerusalem and the surrounding region, as it had been explained to them through Moses. The nations of the Philistines, the Canaanites, the Armenians [!], the Edomites, the Ammonites, and the Moabites fought against them. During that (time), political leadership was entrusted to the elders among them. The Israelites remained in that condition for about four hundred years. They did not have any royal power and were annoyed by attacks from foreign nations. Therefore, they asked God through Samuel, one of their prophets, that He permit them to make someone king over them. Thus, Saul became their king. He defeated the foreign nations and killed Goliath, the ruler of the Philistines. After Saul, David became king, and then Solomon. His kingdom flourished and extended to the borders of the Ḥijâz and further to the borders of the Yemen and to the borders of the land of the Romans (Byzantines). After Solomon, the tribes split into two dynasties. This was in accordance with the necessary consequence of group feeling in dynasties, as we have mentioned before. One of the dynasties was that of the ten tribes in the region of Nablus, the capital of which is Samaria, and the other that of the children of Judah and Benjamin in Jerusalem. Nebuchadnezzar, the king of Babylon, then deprived them of their royal authority. He first (dealt with) the ten tribes in Samaria, and then with the children of Judah in Jerusalem. Their royal authority had had an uninterrupted duration of a thousand years. Now he destroyed their temple, burnt their Torah, and killed their religion. He deported the people to Isfahân and the 'Irâq. Eventually, one of the Persian Kayyanid

(Achaemenid) rulers brought them back to Jerusalem, seventy years after they had left it. They rebuilt the temple and re-established their religion in its original form with priests only. The royal authority belonged to the Persians.

Alexander and the Greeks then defeated the Persians, and the Jews came under Greek domination. The Greek rule then weakened, and, with the help of (their) natural group feeling, the Jews rose against the Greeks and made an end to their domination over them. (Jewish) royal authority was in charge of their Hasmonean priests. (The Hasmoneans) fought the Greeks. Eventually, their power was destroyed. The Romans defeated them, and (the Jews) came under Roman domination. (The Romans) advanced toward Jerusalem, the seat of the children of Herod, relatives by marriage of the Hasmoneans and the last remnant of the Hasmonean dynasty. They laid siege to them for a time, finally conquering (Jerusalem) by force in an orgy of murder, destruction, and arson. They laid Jerusalem in ruins and exiled (the Jews) to Rome and the regions beyond. This was the second destruction of the temple. The Jews call it "the Great Exile." After that, they had no royal authority, because they had lost their group feeling. They remained afterwards under the domination of the Romans and their successors. Their religious affairs were taken care of by their head, called the Kohen.

The Messiah (Jesus) brought (the Jews) his religion, as is known. He abolished some of the laws of the Torah. He performed marvelous wonders, such as healing the insane and reviving the dead. Many people joined him and believed in him. The largest group among his following were his companions, the Apostles. There were twelve of them. He sent some of them as messengers (Apostles) to all parts of the world. They made propaganda for his religious group. That was in the days of Augustus, the first of the Roman emperors, and during the time of Herod, the king of the Jews, who had taken away royal authority from the Hasmoneans, his relatives by marriage. The Jews envied (Jesus) and declared him a liar. Their king, Herod, wrote to the Roman Emperor, Augustus, and incited him against (Jesus). The Roman Emperor gave (the Jews) permission to kill him, and the story of Jesus as recited in the Qur'ân occurred.

The Apostles divided into different groups. Most of them went to the country of the Romans and made propaganda for the Christian religion. Peter was the greatest of them. He settled in Rome, the seat of the Roman emperors. They then wrote down the Gospel that had been revealed to Jesus, in four recensions according to their different traditions. Matthew wrote his Gospel in Jerusalem in Hebrew. It was translated into Latin by John, the son of Zebedee, one of (the Apostles). (The Apostle) Luke wrote his Gospel in Latin for a Roman dignitary. (The Apostle) John, the son of Zebedee, wrote his Gospel in Rome. Peter wrote his Gospel in Latin and ascribed it to his pupil Mark. These four recensions of the Gospel differ from each other. Not all of it is pure revelation, but (the Gospels) have an admixture of the words of Jesus and of the Apostles. Most of (their contents) consists of sermons and stories. There are very few laws in them.

The Apostles came together at that time in Rome and laid down the rules of the Christian community. They entrusted them to Clement, a pupil of Peter, noting in them the list of books that are to be accepted and in accordance with which one must act.

(The books which) belong to the old religious law of the Jews are the following:

The Torah, which consists of five volumes.
The Book of Joshua.
The Book of Judges.
The Book of Ruth.
The Book of Judith.
The four Books of Kings.
The Book of Chronicles.
The three Books of Maccabees, by Ibn Gorion.
The Book of Ezra, the religious leader.
The Book of Esther and the story of Haman.
The Book of Job the Righteous.
The Psalms of David.
The five Books of David's son, Solomon.
The sixteen Prophecies of the major and minor prophets.
The Book of Jesus, the son of Sira, the minister of Solomon.

(The books of) the religious law of Jesus that was received by the Apostles are the following:

The four recensions of the Gospel.
The Book of Paul which consists of fourteen epistles.
The Katholika (General Epistles) which consist of seven epistles, the eighth being the Praxeis (Acts), stories of the Apostles.
The Book of Clement which contains the laws.
The Book of the Apocalypse (Revelation) which contains the vision of John, the son of Zebedee.

The attitude of the Roman emperors toward Christianity varied. At times, they adopted it and honored its adherents. At other times, they did not recognize it and persecuted its adherents and killed and exiled them. Finally, Constantine appeared and adopted Christianity. From then on, all (the Roman emperors) were Christians.

The head of the Christian (community) and the person in charge of (Christian religious) institutions is called Patriarch. He is their religious head and the representative (caliph) of the Messiah among them. He sends his delegates and representatives to the remote Christian nations. They are called "bishop," that is, delegate of the Patriarch. The man who leads the prayers and makes decisions in religious matters is called "priest." The person who withdraws from society and retires into solitude for worship is called "monk." The latter usually seek solitude in (monastic) cells.

The Apostle Peter, the chief Apostle and oldest of the disciples, was in Rome and established the Christian religion there. Nero, the fifth Roman emperor, killed him. Successor to Peter at the Roman see was Arius.

Mark the Evangelist spent seven years in Alexandria and Egypt and the Maghrib making propaganda. After him came Ananias, who was called Patriarch. He was the first Patriarch there. He appointed twelve priests to be with him, and it was arranged that when the Patriarch died, one of the twelve should take his place, and one of the faithful be elected to take his place as the twelfth priest. Thus, the patriarchate fell to the priests.

Later on, dissension broke out among the Christians with regard to the basic principles and articles of their religion. They assembled in Nicea in the days of Constantine, in order to lay down (the doctrine of) true Christianity. Three hundred and eighteen bishops agreed upon one and the same doctrine of Christianity. They wrote it down and called it "the Creed." They made it the fundamental principle to which they would all have reference. Among the things they set down in writing was that with respect to the appointment of the Patriarch as the head of Christianity, no reference should be made to the independent judgment of the priests, as Ananias, the disciple of Mark, had prescribed. That point of view was abolished. The Patriarch was to come from a large group and to be elected by the leaders and chiefs of the believers. It has been so ever since. Later on, other dissensions arose concerning the basic principles of Christianity. Synods concerned with regulating (the religion), were assembled, but there was no dissension with regard to the basic principles (of the method of selecting the Patriarch). It has remained the same ever since.

The Patriarchs always appointed bishops as their delegates. The bishops used to call the Patriarch "Father," as a sign of respect. The priests similarly came to call the bishop "Father," when he was not together with the Patriarch, as a sign of respect. This caused confusion in the use of the title over a long period, ending, it is said, with the Patriarchate of Heraclius in Alexandria. It was considered desirable to distinguish the Patriarch from the bishop in the matter of respect (shown to him by style of address). Therefore, the Patriarch was called "Pope," that is, "Father of fathers." The name (of "Pope") first appeared in Egypt, according to the theory expressed by Jirjis b. al-'Amîd in his *History*. It was then transferred to the occupant of the most important see in (Christianity), the see of Rome, which was the see of the Apostle Peter, as we have mentioned before. The title of Pope has remained characteristic of the see of Rome down to this day.

Thereafter, there were discussions among the Christians with regard to their religion and to Christology. They split into groups and sects, which secured the support of the various Christian rulers against each other. At different times there appeared different sects. Finally, these sects crystallized into three groups, which constitute the (Christian) sects. Others have no significance. These are the Melchites, the Jacobites, and the Nestorians. We do not think that we should blacken the pages of this book with discussions of all their dogmas of unbelief. In general, they are well known. All of them are unbelief. This is clearly stated in the noble Qur'ân. (To) discuss or argue those things with them is not up to us. It is (for them to choose between) conversion to Islam, payment of the poll tax, or death.

Later on, each sect had its own Patriarch. The Patriarch of Rome is today called "Pope." He is of the Melchite persuasion. Rome belongs to the European Christians. Their royal authority is established in that region.

The Patriarch of the (Christian) subjects in Egypt is of the Jacobite persuasion. He resides among them. The Abyssinians follow the religion of (the Egyptian Christians). The Patriarch of Egypt delegates bishops to the Abyssinians, and these bishops arrange religious affairs in Abyssinia. The name of "Pope" is specially reserved for the patriarch of Rome at this time. The Jacobites do not call their patriarch "Pope." The word (Pope) is pronounced *Pappa*.

It is the custom of the Pope with respect to the European Christians to urge them to submit to one ruler and have recourse to him in their disagreements and agreements, in order to avoid the dissolution of the whole thing. His purpose is to have the group feeling that is the strongest among them (concentrated upon one ruler), so that (this ruler) has power over all of them. The ruler is called "Emperor." (The Pope) personally places the crown upon the head of (the emperor), in order to let him have the blessing implied (in that ceremony). The emperor, therefore, is called "the crowned one." Perhaps that is the meaning of the word "emperor." . . .

"God leads astray whomever He wants to lead astray, and He guides whomever He wants to guide."

3 FROM *Paul Wittek*

THE OTTOMAN TURKS—FROM AN EMIRITE OF MARCH WARRIORS TO AN EMPIRE

In this brief article, Paul Wittek sums up the results of his research into the origins of the Ottoman State. He makes it clear that the older view of the Ottomans as a tribe is simply untrue. They were a group of marcher warriors whose basic ideas were modeled on a chivalry and loyalty copied, in part, from Western European knighthood. Their original success was the result of their using trading groups of merchants and artisans to reconstruct the lands they had seized and devastated. Then, thanks to their reliance on the Moslem ulemas or priesthood, they learned to extend tolerance to the Christians they conquered in the Balkans and to recruit some of them into their famous Janissary corps. The result was the great and expanding Ottoman Empire of the mid-fifteenth century.

The conquest of Asia Minor by the Turks was achieved in two stages. Although the Turks, towards the end of the eleventh century, had overrun the whole of Asia Minor, yet they were able to keep only

SOURCE. Paul Wittek, *The Rise of the Ottoman Empire* (London: Royal Asiatic Society of Great Britain and Ireland, 1965), pp. 33–51. Reprinted by permission of the publisher and the author.

the central and eastern parts of the peninsula. It was not till fully
200 years later, towards the end of the thirteenth century, that they
became, by a second invasion, the lords of western Asia Minor also.
Both invasions were comparable neither to a well-planned military
occupation on the part of a conquering state, nor to the invasions
of nomadic people. On the contrary, both were the outcome of a
long existing tension, resulting from the increasing growth of the
offensive power of the Turks and the continual decrease in the
defensive forces of the Byzantines. A breach in the frontier dam gave
a free inlet to long pent-up floods. Nomadic Turks, who still
retained their tribal system, took part in both invasions—that is,
they followed the conquerors into the land after its subjugation.
But in both cases they played a subordinate part in comparison with
the Ghāzīs, those march-warriors who for generations had attacked
and overrun the frontier and had become familiar with the country
of their future conquests; it was these Ghāzīs who led and largely
achieved the conquests. And naturally the leaders of the Ghāzīs
became the princes of the emirates which were founded in the newly
conquered lands.

. . . . .

There sprang up in western Asia Minor, in the second half of the
thirteenth century, a number of Ghāzī emirates, established in the
conquered lands. Among these was the emirate of Osman, the
nucleus from which the Ottoman Empire later developed. In
investigating the historical tradition of the origin of the Ottomans,
we come to the conclusion that the oldest and best tradition, the one
which stands the test of historical criticism, clearly shows the
Ottomans as Ghāzīs and their chiefs as leaders of an ever-growing
and powerful Ghāzī organization. . . . The other emirates of western
Asia Minor were also Ghāzī emirates. Not one of them shows any
trace whatever of tribal consciousness or of tribal origin; every one
of them originated from the Ghāzī organization which had conquered the respective district and had as ruler its chief, who became
the founder of the dynasty.

At first the Ottomans played a very modest part among the other
emirates and we know from an outline . . . of the political structure
of Anatolia during the fourteenth century that the Ghāzī character
of the Ottoman state was not peculiar to it alone, but that quite a
number of other emirates also owed their origin to the Ghāzī movement and continued its traditions.

What, then, are these Ghāzī traditions ? . . . We know that the Ghāzīs acknowledged the *futuwwa*. The futuwwa, to give a brief explanation, was a canon of rules by means of which the virtuous life, as understood by Islam with its mystical inclination, might be lived. Various Islamic corporations were based on the futuwwa, which they took as their moral guide. For instance, in addition to the Ghāzīs, we find a futuwwa corporation called Akhīs, which was a brotherhood consisting of artisans and merchants. These futuwwa corporations were reorganized about 1200 by the caliph Nāsir. This last great 'Abbasid bent all his energies to restoring the secular power of the caliphate and organizing Islam against the attacks of the Crusaders. His regulation of the futuwwa probably served the same ends and aimed at marshalling all those forces which were of military importance and attaching them to the person of the caliph. Doubtless the guilds of artisans had military potentiality, but of far greater importance were the proper military organizations, led by their own leaders, the emirs. This element, socially and racially distinct from the rest of the population, obviously had to be organized in a corporation of a more chivalrous kind. The corporations of Ghāzīs admirably supplied the required qualities, and were excellently adapted to the programme of the caliph by reason of what was already their dominating idea—namely, war against the unbelievers. And, from the time of the caliph Nāsir onwards, the title of Ghāzī was held by powerful princes of Syria and northern Mesopotamia, both countries which in the time of the Crusaders had become frontier districts, threatened by the Christians. These princes were bound to the caliph by the bonds of the futuwwa, which imposed on both the follower and the "senior" ("seigneur") the obligation of mutual fidelity. Similar bonds evidently existed within the corporation between the emir and his "knights." Thus the popular Ghāzī movement, which in that time of struggle against the Crusaders found a sure response also in the centres of Islam and inevitably increased in prestige, became now, in Syria and Mesopotamia, an institution comparable to the European knighthood. In the far-off Anatolian marches the Ghāzī movement doubtlessly remained a popular one. But, even so, many of the features that were characteristic of knighthood must have been inherent in this popular movement, and sooner or later some influences of the Ghāzī knighthood evolved in the Old Moslem countries could not fail to appear and to strengthen these features. In any case we have a whole array of facts showing that among the

Ghāzīs of Anatolia there were current certain ideas, customs and bonds which on the one hand make clear their connection with the futuwwa, and on the other hand indicate that the Ghāzī of Anatolia, or at least the leading elements among them, felt that they were a group, linked together by special bonds. . . . We are told how one of the emirs of the house of Aydīn was designated as "Sultan of the Ghāzīs" by the shaikh of the Mevlevī darvish order. From the hands of the shaikh he received the latter's war-club, which he laid on his own head and said: "With this club will I first subdue all my passions and then kill all enemies of the faith." This ceremony means that the emir accepted the shaikh as his "senior," and his words show that the quality of Ghāzī also involved ethical obligations. Lastly, the conferring of a personal weapon by the senior corresponds to a well-known regulation of the ceremonial canon of the futuwwa. 'Ashiqpashazade, an Ottoman historian of the fifteenth century, tells a legendary tale the real meaning of which was no longer understood at his time. In this tale, Ghāzī Osman presents to one of his lieges, on the occasion of the granting of a fief, his own sword and a drinking-cup. Here we again have the presentation of a personal weapon. But the cup is certainly a survival of a Ghāzī ceremony, for we know that the cup plays an important part in the rites of the futuwwa. We know, further, that the Ghāzīs distinguished themselves from the rest of the population by a special head-dress, a white cap, introduced among the Ghāzīs of the western Anatolian marches towards the end of the thirteenth century and retained by the Ottomans until very late. These examples will suffice. We may be sure that the title of Ghāzī, held by certain emirs and avoided by others, was used with the intention of expressing the peculiar character and tendency of a state whose ruler was a Ghāzī.

A ghāzī state was a body which aimed at military conquest. The chief had the allegiance of his followers in return for the obligation to provide them with the means of livelihood, which meant the acquisition of booty. At the time of its foundation a Ghāzī state was so entirely composed of the warrior elements that it at first lacked the elements necessary for the organization and utilization of the conquered territory, such as clergy, peasants, artisans, merchants. The country, after having suffered much through its conquest, was rapidly drained of its resources, and new conquests, or at least raids, soon became necessary. It was only when these conquests or raids came to a stop, and the conquerors were forced to fall back on their own resources, that they were faced with the task of reconstructing and organizing their country. Since they themselves had not the elements necessary for this purpose, they were forced to attract such elements into their land from outside. The only Ghāzī state which succeeded in solving this problem was that of the Ottomans. The rest fell back, after a short period of prosperity, the period of successful raids, into insignificance and weakness, and this decline was accompanied and accelerated by internal feuds, the same fate which had befallen the Danishmends in the twelfth century, 200 years before.

What was it that preserved the Ottomans from a similar fate? I give the answer in advance: it was above all the tenacious resistance with which the Byzantines opposed them, a resistance which indeed was imperative against an enemy who threatened the immediate neighbourhood of their capital. While the armed expeditions which the Byzantines had dispatched from time to time against the other western emirates had already ceased—it was in 1304 that the last, that of the Catalan Company, was sent—and while these emirates had already consolidated their conquests the Ghāzīs of Osman had hardly achieved their first and very modest successes; for they were held up by a defensive system which here, in the immediate neighbourhood of the capital, was carefully maintained, and which included such strongholds as Nicæa, to whose assistance the whole imperial army could be brought in a few hours.

But in the struggle with this extraordinary resistance the Ghāzī state of Osman developed its extraordinary strength. The grave sternness and tenacious courage which distinquish this state in its later history were deeply imprinted upon its soul during these years of its early youth. During this long period of fighting the Ghāzīs of Osman were joined by all those hosts of warriors who, in the other emirates with definitely established frontiers, found no further occupation. In this way the small state of the Ottomans disposed of disproportionally large war forces, and its dynamic power was thus tremendously increased. In comparison with the rate of the conquests in western Anatolia, success seemed at first to come very slowly: Brusa did not fall until 1326, Nicæa fell in 1331. Then, at about 1340, almost everything that could possibly be seized from the Byzantines in Asia Minor was conquered. Only a few towns on the coast in close proximity to the capital still held out. An attack on the capital itself, whose mighty walls and buildings arose on the other side of the Bosphorus, could not yet be dreamed of. So there was of necessity a pause.

During this interval of respite the frontiers of the emirate were probably extended eastward into the interior, where Mongol rule was rapidly declining. But, above all, they took advantage of this pause to settle down in the conquered regions. As we have emphasized, the Ghāzīs had in general very largely adapted themselves to the districts which they had conquered. This is especially true of the Ottomans, who had to confront the Byzantine Akritai for a period of half a century longer than the Turks of the other Ghāzī emirates. Owing to the slow advance of their conquest they had ample time to settle down in their newly acquired possessions and to make use of them. When they seized the fairly large towns of Bithynia and its fertile plains, they already possessed the experience with which to administer such a country. The fact that the Ottomans had in such large measure adapted themselves to the civilization of the country which they attacked made it all the easier for the Akritai to join them in groups, and for the forts and smaller towns to capitulate voluntarily. In view of the difficulty of their task, peaceful conquests of this kind and any increase in their forces were welcome to the Ottomans, and they certainly did everything to promote desertion among their adversaries. From the fact that a detachment of Catalans joined them in 1305, we see that even totally alien elements entered their ranks. The famous Ottoman Ghāzī family Mikhaloghlu ("Michaelsons"), which still exists at the present day, never forgot that they were the descendants of a Christian renegade who had joined Osman.

Nor must we forget that the Ottomans were situated closer to the districts of Seljuk urban culture than any of the remaining Ghāzī emirates. At a short distance to their rear lay Eskishehir, the ancient Doryleum, a town on the important trade route Konia–Constantinople, which led, moreover, through the Ottoman territory. This connection with the Moslem hinterland is of the greatest importance, for only this hinterland was capable of providing the Ottomans with the elements indispensable for the organization and utilization of the conquered lands. It has quite rightly been pointed out that the Akhīs already appear in the first period of the Ottoman state as an important element. You may recall that the Akhīs were guilds of artisans and merchants, organized on the basis of the futuwwa. The presence of Akhīs shows that at a very early date numerous urban elements had joined the Ottomans from the hinterland. Of still greater importance are the 'ulemā, the Moslem clergy, who represented the forces capable of developing an administrative system.

Immediately after the conquest of Brusa and Nicæa, schools of theology (medreses) were erected in these towns. This proves that the 'ulemā had already acquired a strong position in the Ottoman state. The early intervention of the 'ulemā is also of importance in another way: together with the Old Moslem governmental traditions they brought the principle of tolerance towards Christians and Jews, which was closely connected with their financial policy, based on the payment of tribute by the non-Moslems in return for this toleration. Thus they exercised a very necessary influence over the Ghāzī state. For although the Ghāzīs were very tolerant regarding the civilization of the conquered country, they themselves having long since taken root in that civilization, yet they were and remained the relentless "warriors of the faith," continually incited by fanatical dervishes to force Islam upon the inhabitants of the conquered country. We may say that while a breach in the civilization was avoided thanks to the Ghāzī character of the conquerers, it is due to the early intervention of the 'ulemā that this civilization could continue to exist under the preserving forms of the old creed. This was especially the case in the towns, where the influence of the 'ulemā was predominant.

But the Ottoman inscription of 1337 on the mosque at Brusa . . . shows us how strongly the leaders of this state felt themselves to be Ghāzīs. The pause which set in after the conquest of Bithynia had been accomplished could only be a short one. Hosts of Ghāzīs, attracted by the fame of the new conquests, poured in ever-increasing numbers into the Ottoman state, and it was necessary to keep them occupied. A passing expedient was offered by the internal struggles in the Byzantine Empire: the Ottomans sent in 1345 large contingents to Thrace to aid the Emperor John VI Cantacuzenus against his rival John V Palæologus. The Byzantines had formerly drawn their auxiliary troops from the coastal emirates, mainly from Aydîn. But the latter was just then engaged in struggles with the forces of the Union of the Christian Levant powers, which had entrenched themselves in Smyrna. Therefore Cantacuzenus now turned to his Ottoman neighbour, and in so doing he recognized him as master of Bithynia, and even gave him his daughter in marriage. This interlude was of the greatest importance: the Ghāzīs, returning from this expedition with rich spoil, made it clear to the Ottoman ruler in which direction lay his future conquests. The goal was Thrace and Macedonia, the way led over the Dardanelles and the peninsula of Gallipoli. Separated from the

Dardanelles by the Ghāzī emirate of Karasî, the Ottomans took advantage of the fact that the latter had already entered upon a phase of external weakness and internal dissension, and seized it. Shortly afterwards the Ottoman troops in the service of Cantacuzenus were given a stronghold on Gallipoli by the emperor, and, a little later, after the great earthquake of 1354, this became the base for their occupation of the whole Gallipoli peninsula, the starting-point for their further expeditions into the Balkans.

But, before the Ottomans undertook these conquering expeditions in the West, they extended their eastern Anatolian possessions. In 1354, the same year in which they settled in the peninsula of Gallipoli, they succeeded in taking Angora, the first large town with the characteristics of the old Seljuk civilization. A coin struck in that town shows that until shortly before this, at least until 1343, the brilliantly organized administration of the Mongol (but naturally long since Iranized) Ilkhans had been operative there. Angora was a town of wholesale merchants and industrial citizens, and was a centre of Akhī corporations. Such penetration into Asia Minor procured to the Ghāzī state those urban elements which it needed for the organization of its conquests. But this turning against Asia Minor, together with the annexation of the emirate of Karasî, had, of course, shown the Anatolian emirs very clearly the menace which the Ottoman state held for them. The Ottoman emir Murad I, succeeding his father, Orkhan, in 1362, had to begin his reign by securing these newly acquired lands against a coalition headed by the emir of Karaman. With the help of his experienced and numerous warriors Murad soon subdued his adversary and extended his power as far as Tokat, an old town with Danishmend reminiscences. There he ordered the history of that Ghāzī dynasty to be written down in Turkish, from the Persian work composed 150 years before by order of the Seljuk sultan Alaeddin Kaiqobad I; he may have become interested in this through the songs and stories which dealt with the Danishmends and were current among his own Ghāzīs. Later on, Murad had more than once again to fight the Karamans and their allied emirs, and he always returned victorious and with additional gains of Anatolian territory. But he also systematically increased his Anatolian possessions by peaceful methods. The bride of his son Bayezid, a princess of Germain, brought as dowry in 1381 a large part of this emirate, including its capital Kutahya. Later Murad bought almost all the lands of another neighbour emirate, that of Hamid. He was indeed able to do this, for he was immensely wealthy by reason of the enormous booty brought home by the Ghāzīs from their raids in the West.

For, since about 1360, the invasion of the Balkans was in full swing. Again the Ghāzīs pushed forward the frontiers of Islam. As in the eleventh century this frontier had been moved from the Taurus and Euphrates to the western border of central Anatolia, and had advanced during the thirteenth century up to the Aegean Sea, in the same way now, in the fourteenth century, it was pushed on into the Balkans and successively carried further up to the Adriatic coast and the edge of the Alps. Only these actions were no longer spontaneously undertaken by independent Ghāzī hosts, but were deliberate and well-organized state enterprises. The state now had in its possession the equipment necessary for these expeditions, such as an army and an administrative executive. Yet it always felt it was a state of Ghāzīs serving the idea of the holy war, and it actually was now the Ghāzī state κατ'ἐξοχήν. The fact that the Ottoman emirate remained the only real Ghāzī state, the exclusively active and successful representative of the Ghāzī movement, whose renown spread far beyond its own borders, attracted the entire warlike youth of Anatolia and all those elements who were full of enthusiasm for religious war, for adventure, fame and spoil. The "potentiel militaire" of this state was always larger than its own circumference, in spite of the rapid growth of the latter. Thus this state must conquer, it must continue the ghazā, the religious war. The renown of its exploits increased with the extent of its conquests and attracted continually increasing numbers of volunteers from still more remote districts. While the Ottoman state continually grew in power and in size, the other emirates were fading away, for their warriors were drawn towards those places where they were sure of finding employment. In their weakness they felt the day drawing near when they would fall an easy prey. They therefore united round the strongest among themselves, the Karaman. The desperate attempts of these coalitions to escape their impending fate gave the Ottomans a pretext, and even compelled them to strike the final blow at these emirates.

In 1400 they had incorporated them all and were masters of almost the whole of Anatolia. By that time they had taken nearly all the European possessions of Byzantium, and there remained only Constantinople, rising with its thousand-year-old walls as an island amidst the Turkish floods. Bulgaria, too, had been conquered and Serbia reduced to a small part of her former territory, and even this rest was brought under Turkish suzerainty. The Turkish armies were already fighting in Bosnia, Albania, in the Peloponnesus and Wallachia; Turkish Ghāzī raiders had penetrated into Hungary and the alpine valleys of Styria. Turkish pirate ships undertook daring raids into the Aegean Sea, defying the strongest fleet of those times, that of the Venetians. A century had passed since Christendom had lost its last possessions in the Holy Land, and now it saw itself menaced by the Moslems in the very heart of Europe. An army of knights, in whose ranks were the King of Hungary and a grandson of the French king, was sent out by the West to meet this danger, and it was literally annihilated in Bulgaria, near Nicopolis on the Danube, in 1396. After this victory Bayezid entertained the most daring plans. He held Constantinople besieged with one of his armies, while he himself attacked eastern Anatolia and is said to have contemplated the conquest of Syria. Surely, was not this state already an empire?

History itself has answered this question in the negative. The conquests in the Moslem East, undertaken with so much energy by the Ottoman state, now brought it into conflict with another force. Timur, whose ambition was directed to the creation of a large empire in the Old Moslem world, was determined to crush this rivalry at its very beginning. In 1401 he penetrated as far as Angora, where he destroyed the army of Bayezid and took the latter prisoner. The circumstances under which this defeat took place are very significant: during the battle entire local contingents of the Ottoman army deserted to the enemy. Just as significant were the consequences of this defeat: the emirates of Asia Minor were restored and regained their independence, and the remaining Ottoman territory was broken up into several parts. All this clearly shows that the structure of the Ottoman state was still a very unstable one, and that the imperial ideal had not yet succeeded in taking root. An empire, as Bayezid planned it, was only the premature dream of an audacious ambition. Not only did Bayezid overlook the fact that his state still lacked internally all that was necessary for the establishment of an empire, but he also failed to perceive the real direction in which the development towards an empire lay, the direction followed by his predecessors with unerring instinct. The propitious harmony which had up till then existed between the Ghāzī movement and the traditions of the Old Moslem world, between the conquest of Christian countries and extension towards the Mohammedan East, was lost under Bayezid. Both his internal and external policy abandoned the traditions of the Ghāzīs and displayed a unilateral inclination towards Islam. The 'ulemā, now too numerous and too powerful, not only succeeded in winning over the sultan to the more subtle habits, pleasures, and arts of High Islam, but also to their views on the organization of the state. This they now endeavoured to fashion according to Old Moslem traditions, much too fast and without regard to the existing conditions. Above all, the 'ulemā converted the sultan to their ideas of external policy, which naturally concerned the countries of High Islam, which were their spiritual home. It was this which led to the conflict with Timur and to the catastrophe of Angora. The behaviour of Timur after his victory was remarkable. Though he stayed for several months in Anatolia, he had no intention of incorporating it into his state, but aimed only to re-establish the Ghāzī emirates which had been annexed by Bayezid. The remaining Ottoman possessions he left untouched. There was only one more warlike act which he achieved in Anatolia: he conquered Smyrna, which had been held by the Franks since the days of Ghāzī Umur Beg. After this he withdrew. Timur's behaviour must be understood as a demonstration to the public opinion of Islam that by his intervention in Asia Minor he desired nothing more than to recall to the Ottomans their real task—that is, the Ghāzī idea, which they were beginning to renounce. By achieving himself a deed worthy of a Ghāzī in taking Smyrna, he thought to win the approbation of the entire Moslem world. In this way the Ottoman state was saved by the prestige which it possessed as a Ghāzī state.

Its next task was to re-establish the unity of the state, which had been divided up among the sons of Bayezid. During those years of dismemberment it became clear that the Balkan provinces could not exist without the territories of Asia Minor and *vice versa*. The reunited Ottoman state once more openly recognized the Ghāzī movement as its leading idea. The restoration of the Anatolian emirates by Timur directed the Ottomans again to the Balkans as their principal field of action. The capital is therefore moved from Brusa, the "city of the theologians," to Adrianopolis, the "city of the Ghāzīs." But Anatolia was not lost to view, since its importance as a connecting link with the Old Moslem world had been clearly understood. The alternating movements of conquest in the West and extension towards the East soon begins again. But this time progress is made at a slower, more patient and more balanced pace, which shows that the Ottoman leaders knew how to weigh the forces and had understood the fundamental principles of their state. The Anatolian emirates were again annexed one after the other, but now step by step, avoiding any appearance of deliberate conquest.

With regard to the European possessions, an important problem still remained to be solved. The Turks called this land "Rūmili," meaning in this case the "land of the Greek Christians." The conquest of this land had been only to a small extent the achievement of the Ghāzīs; the large territories of the kingdoms of Bulgaria and Serbia and of the different principalities in the south of peninsula had been acquired through the well-planned campaigns of the Ottoman army—that is, through state expeditions—and had also been immediately placed under the administration of the state. Conversion to Islam had been practised only in those regions which were conquered by the Ghāzīs—that is, in Eastern Thrace, which was taken at first, and then again later in the furthest western frontiers, in Albania and Bosnia, where again a long-disputed frontier district, a Ghāzī march, came into existence—the vast territory between these two Ghāzī zones was allowed to remain Christian, thanks to the principle of toleration inherent in Moslem governmental traditions. This was financially, as we have seen, of great advantage. But on the other hand it had the grave disadvantage that the larger part of the population of the state was lost for the most important institutions of the state, the political government, the administration and the army. At about 1430 this problem too was solved by Murad II, and this in complete accord with the fundamental tendencies of the state: the custom was introduced of regularly taking military recruits from the Christian subjects while they were still boys, they were forced to become Mohammedans and sent to special educational institutions, where they were Turkicized and brought up mostly for the army, but those who showed greater talents were educated for service at court or as state officials. In this way two fundamental tendencies of the Ghāzī movement, conversion to Islam and the absorption of indigenous elements, were definitely incorporated in a state institution. We mean the corps of the Janissaries; it had already existed before, but until then had consisted of boys captured by the Ghāzīs in the lands which they raided. Now, by the regular recruiting in their own provinces, this institution became one of the strongest pillars of the Ottoman state and meant much more than a regiment of guards in the army; it was the institution in which the very best elements of the

native population were brought up to become the most faithful and
devoted servants of the state. Owing to this institution, the indigenous Christian population furnished to the state its greatest
statesmen and military commanders. The representatives of the Old
Moslem traditions, the 'ulemā, had now found their counterpoise.
Moreover, the Old Moslem science and arts were no longer the
exclusive spiritual content of the society: we notice at that time the
"romantic" movement, which we have mentioned as a national one
in the first lecture, and which was especially interested in what we
may call "Turkish antiquities." Murad II, the restorer of the state,
thought his creation so far stabilized that he retired to Manissa,
leaving to his advisers both the affairs of state and the charge of his
son Mehmed II, a boy of fourteen years. Murad II, who had made
it his life's work to make good the damage that had been done by
the bold ambition of Bayezid, was himself doubtless cool towards
the imperial idea. But how far the latter had already taken root
around him is shown by the theory of the Turkish writers of that
time, according to which the Ottomans were the descendants of the
eldest Oghuz grandson Qayï, who was called upon to rule the
world. Mehmed II grew up amidst the imperial ideas of this milieu,
and his first action, the conquest of Constantinople, aimed at its
achievement.

4 FROM

Sir Steven Runciman

THE FALL OF CONSTANTINOPLE

Among the important events that took place during the long history of Western European–Moslem relations was the Fall of Constantinople. Although it had long been clear that Constantinople could not endure as an island in a Turkish sea, its actual conquest sent a shiver of horror through a Western Europe which had done little to avert the disaster. Then, for the next two centuries, the same Europe had to deal with the aggressive advances of an Ottoman Empire which had made the Byzantine Imperial capital its own. For a stirring account of this fall, told by a leading historian of the Byzantine world, Sir Steven Runciman, the following pages are a must. They explain in detail Byzantium's last days and the immediate results of its fall to the Islamic forces of Mohammed II, the Conqueror.

As the siege continued in the city the bells of the churches rang and their wooden gongs sounded as icons and relics were brought out upon the shoulders of the faithful and carried round through the streets along the length of the walls, pausing to bless with their holy presence the spots where the damage was greatest and the danger most pressing; and the throng that followed behind them, Greeks and Italians, Orthodox and Catholic, sang hymns and repeated the Kyrie Eleison. The Emperor himself came to join in the procession; and when it was ended he summonded his notables and commanders, Greek and Italian, and spoke to them. His speech was recorded by two men present, his secretary Phrantzes and the Archbishop of Mitylene. Each of them wrote down the Emperor's speech in his own way, adding pedantic allusions and pious aphorisms, to give it a rhetorical form that in all probability it lacked. But their accounts agree sufficiently for us to know its substance. Constantine told his hearers that the great assault was about to begin. To his Greek subjects he said that a man should always be ready to die either for his faith or for his country or for his family or for his sovereign. Now his people must be prepared to die for all four causes. He spoke of the glories and the high traditions

SOURCE. Sir Steven Runciman, *The Fall of Constantinople, 1453* (New York: Cambridge University Press, 1965), pp. 130–169. Reprinted by permission of the publisher.

of the great Imperial city. He spoke of the perfidy of the infidel Sultan who had provoked the war in order to destroy the True Faith and to put his false prophet in the seat of Christ. He urged them to remember that they were the descendants of the heroes of ancient Greece and Rome and to be worthy of their ancestors. For his part, he said, he was ready to die for his faith, his city, and his people. He then turned to the Italians, thanking them for the great services that they had rendered and telling of his trust in them for the fighting that was to come. He begged them all, Greeks and Italians alike, not to fear the vast numbers of the enemy and the barbarous devices of fire and of noise designed to alarm them. Let their spirits be high; let them be brave and steadfast. With the help of God they would be victorious

All that were present rose to assure the Emperor that they were ready to sacrifice their lives and their homes for him. He then walked slowly round the chamber, asking each one of them to forgive him if ever he had caused offence. They followed his example, embracing one another, as men do who expect to die.

The day was nearly over. Already crowds were moving towards the great Church of the Holy Wisdom. For the past five months no pious Greek had stepped through its portals to hear the Sacred Liturgy defiled by Latins and by renegades. But on that evening the bitterness was ended. Barely a citizen, except for the soldiers on the walls, stayed away from this desperate service of intercession. Priests who held union with Rome to be a mortal sin now came to the altar to serve with their Unionist brothers. The Cardinal was there, and beside him bishops who would never acknowledge his authority; and all the people came to make confession and take communion, not caring whether Orthodox or Catholic administered it. There were Italians and Catalans along with the Greeks. The golden mosaics, studded with the images of Christ and His Saints and the Emperors and Empresses of Byzantium, glimmered in the light of a thousand lamps and candles; and beneath them for the last time the priests in their splendid vestments moved in the solemn rhythm of the Liturgy. At this moment there was union in the Church of Constantinople.

When the Emperor's Council was dismissed the ministers and commanders rode through the city to join in the worship. After confessing and taking communion each then went to his station, resolved to conquer or to die. When Giustiniani and his Greek and

Italian comrades came to their allotted places and passed through
the inner wall to the outer wall and the stockade, orders were given
for the gates of the inner wall to be closed behind them, that there
might be no retreat.

Later in the evening the Emperor himself rode on his Arab mare
to the great cathedral and made his peace with God. Then he returned through the dark streets to his Palace at Blachernae and
summoned his household. Of them, as he had done of his ministers,
he asked forgiveness for any unkindness that he might have shown
them, and he bade them good-bye. It was close on midnight when
he mounted his horse again and rode, accompanied by the faithful
Phrantzes, down the length of the land-walls, to see that everything
was in order and that the gates through the inner wall were closed.
On their way back to Blachernae the Emperor dismounted near the
Caligarin Gate and took Phrantzes with him up a tower, at the out-
most angle of the Blachernae wall, from which they could peer out
into the darkness both ways, across to the Mesoteichion on the left
and down to the Golden Horn on the right. Below them they could
hear noises as the enemy brought up their guns over the filled-in
foss. This activity had been going on since sunset, so the watchmen
told them. In the distance they could see flickering lights as the
Turkish ships moved across the Golden Horn. Phrantzes waited
with his master for an hour or so. Then Constantine dismissed him;
and they never met again. The battle was beginning.

The afternoon of Monday, 28 May, had been clear and bright.
As the sun began to sink towards the western horizon it shone
straight into the faces of the defenders on the walls, almost blind-
ing them. It was then that the Turkish camp had sprung into
activity. Men came forward in thousands to complete the filling of
the foss, while others brought up cannons and war-machines. The
sky clouded over soon after sunset, and there was a heavy shower
of rain; but the work went on uninterrupted, and the Christians
could do nothing to hinder it. At about half-past one in the morning the Sultan judged that everything was ready and gave the order
for the assault.

. . . . .

There was not time for prayer at the walls. The Sultan had made
his plans with care. Despite his arrogant words to his army experience had taught him to respect the enemy. On this occasion he
would wear them down before risking his best troops in the battle.

It was his irregulars, the Bashi-bazouks, whom he first sent forward. There were many thousands of them, adventurers from every country and race, many of them Turks but many more from Christian countries, Slavs, Hungarians, Germans, Italians and even Greeks, all of them ready enough to fight against their fellow-Christians in view of the pay that the Sultan gave them and the booty that he promised. Most of them provided their own arms, which were an odd assortment of scimitars and slings, bows and a few arquebuses; but a large number of scaling-ladders had been distributed amongst them. They were unreliable troops, excellent at their first onrush but easily discouraged if they were not at once successful. Knowing this weakness Mehmet placed behind them a line of military police, armed with thongs and maces, whose orders were to urge them on and to strike and chastise any who showed signs of wavering. Behind the military police were the Sultan's own Janissaries. If any frightened irregular made his way through the police they were to cut him down with their scimitars.

The Bashi-bazouks' attack was launched all along the line, but it was only pressed hard in the Lycus valley. Elsewhere the walls were too strong; and they were attacked chiefly with the purpose of distracting the defenders from going to re-inforce their comrades in the vital section. There the fighting was fierce. The Bashi-bazouks were up against soldiers far better armed and far better trained than themselves; and they were further handicapped by their numbers. They were continually in each other's way. Stones hurled against them could kill or disable many at a time. Though a few attempted to retreat, most of them kept on, fixing their ladders to the walls and the stockade and clambering up, only to be cut down before they reached the top. Giustiniani and his Greeks and Italians were supplied with all the muskets and culverins that could be found in the city. The Emperor came himself to encourage them. After nearly two hours of fighting Mehmet ordered the Bashi-bazouks to retire. They had been checked and repulsed, but they had served their purpose in wearing the enemy.

. . . . .

The Turks had been no more successful on other sectors. Along the southern stretch of the land-walls Ishak was able to keep up enough pressure to prevent the defence from moving men to the Lycus valley, but, with his own best troops gone to fight there, he could not make a serious attack. Along the Marmora Hamza Bey had difficulty in bringing his ships close in shore. The few landing parties that he was able to send were easily repulsed by the monks to whom the defence had been entrusted or by Prince Orthan and his followers. There were feints along the whole line of the Golden Horn but no real attempt at an assault. Around the Blachernae quarter the fighting was fiercer. On the low ground by the harbour the troops that Zaganos had brought across the bridge kept up a constant attack, as did Karadja Pasha's men higher up the slope. But Minotto and his Venetians were able to hold their section of the walls against Zaganos, and the Bocchiardi brothers against Karadja.

The Sultan was said to be indignant at the failure of his Anatolians. But it is probable that he intended them, like the irregulars before them, to wear out the enemy rather than themselves to enter the city. He had promised a great prize to the first soldier who should successfully break through the stockade; and he wished the privilege to go to some member of his own favourite regiment, his Janissaries. The time had now come for them to enter the battle. He was anxious; for if they failed it would scarcely be possible to continue the siege. He gave his orders quickly. Before the Christians had time to refresh themselves and do more than a few rough repairs to the stockade, a rain of missiles, arrows, javelins, stones and bullets, fell upon them; and behind the rain, the Janissaries advanced at the double, not rushing in wildly as the Bashi-bazouks and the Anatolians had done, but keeping their ranks in perfect order, unbroken by the missiles of the enemy. The martial music that urged them on was so loud that the sound could be heard between the roar of the guns from right across the Bosphorus. Mehmet himself led them as far as the foss and stood there shouting encouragement as they passed him. Wave after wave of these fresh, magnificent and stoutly armoured men rushed up to the stockade, to tear at the barrels of earth that surmounted it, to hack at the beams that supported it, and to place their ladders against it where it could not be brought down, each wave making way without panic for its successor. The Christians were exhausted. They had fought with only a few minutes' respite for more than four hours; but they fought with desperation, knowing that if they gave way it would be the end. Behind them in the city the church bells were clanging again, and a great murmur of prayer rose to heaven.

The fighting along the stockade was hand-to-hand now. For an hour or so the Janissaries could make no headway. The Christians began to think that the onslaught was weakening a little. But fate was against them. At the corner of the Blachernae wall, just before it joined the double Theodosian wall, there was, half-hidden by a tower, a small sally-port known as the Kerkoporta. It had been closed up many years earlier; but old men remembered it. Just before the siege began it had been reopened, to allow sorties into the enemy's flank. During the fighting the Bochiardis and their men had made effective use of it against Karadja Pasha's troops. But now someone returning from a sortie forgot to bar the little gate after him. Some Turks noticed the opening and rushed through it into the courtyard behind it and began to climb up a stairway leading to the top of the wall. The Christians who were just outside the gate saw what was happening and crowded back to retake control of it and to prevent other Turks from following. In the confusion some fifty Turks were left inside the wall, where they could have been surrounded and eliminated if at that moment a worse disaster had not occurred.

It was just before sunrise that a shot fired at close range from a culverin struck Giustiniani and pierced his breastplate. Bleeding copiously and obviously in great pain, he begged his men to take him off the battle-field. One of them went to the Emperor who was fighting near by to ask for the key of a little gate that led through the inner wall. Constantine hurried to his side to plead with him not to desert his post. But Giustiniani's nerve was broken; he insisted on flight. The gate was opened, and his bodyguard carried him into the city, through the streets down to the harbour where they placed him on a Genoese ship. His troops noticed his going. Some of them may have thought that he had retreated to defend the inner wall; but most of them concluded that the battle was lost. Someone shouted out in terror that the Turks had crossed the wall. Before the little gate could be shut again the Genoese streamed headlong through it. The Emperor and his Greeks were left on the field alone.

From across the foss the Sultan noticed the panic. Crying: "The city is ours," he ordered the Janissaries to charge again and beckoned on a company led by a giant called Hasan. Hasan hacked his way over the top of the broken stockade and was deemed to have won the promised prize. Some thirty Janissaries followed him. The Greeks fought back. Hasan himself was forced to his knees by a blow from a stone and slain; and seventeen of his comrades perished with him. But the remainder held their positions on the stockade; and many more Janissaries crowded to join them. The Greeks resisted tenaciously. But the weight of numbers forced them back to the inner wall. In front of it was another ditch which had been deepened in places to provide earth for reinforcing the stockade. Many of the Greeks were forced back into these holes and could not easily clamber out, with the great inner wall rising behind them. The Turks who were now on top of the stockade fired down on them and massacred them. Soon many of the Janissaries reached the inner wall and climbed up it unopposed. Suddenly someone looked up and saw Turkish flags flying from the tower above the Kerkoporta. The cry went up: "The city is taken."

While he was pleading with Giustiniani the Emperor had been told of the Turks' entry through the Kerkoporta. He rode there at once, but he came too late. Panic had spread to some of the Genoese there. In the confusion it was impossible to close the gate. The Turks came pouring through; and the Bocchiardis' men were too few now to push them back. Constantine turned his horse and galloped back to the Lycus valley and the breaches in the stockade. With him was the gallant Spaniard who claimed to be his cousin, Don Francisco of Toledo, and his own cousin Theophilus Palaeologus and a faithful comrade-at-arms, John Dalmata. Together they tried to rally the Greeks, in vain; the slaughter had been too great. They dismounted and for a few minutes the four of them held the approach to the gate through which Giustiniani had been carried. But the defence was broken now. The gate was jammed with Christian soldiers trying to make their escape, as more and more Janissaries fell on them. Theophilus shouted that he would rather die than live and disappeared into the oncoming hordes. Constantine himself knew now that the Empire was lost, and he had no wish to survive it. He flung off his imperial insignia and, with Don Francisco and John Dalmata still at his side, he followed Theophilus. He was never seen again.

. . . . .

Signals reporting the entry through the walls were flashed round the whole Turkish army. The Turkish ships in the Golden Horn hastened to land their men on the foreshore and to attack the harbour walls. They met with little resistance, except by the Horaia Gate, near the Aivan Serai of today. There the companies of two Cretan ships blockaded themselves in three towers and refused to surrender. Elsewhere the Greeks had fled to their homes in the hope

of protecting their families, and the Venetians took to their ships.
It was not long before a company of Turks had forced their way
through the Plataea Gate, at the foot of the valley still dominated
by the great aqueduct of Valens. Another company came through
the Horaia Gate. Wherever they entered detachments were sent
along within the walls to fling open other gates for their comrades
who were waiting outside. Nearby, seeing that all was lost, local
fishermen opened the gates of the Petrion quarter themselves, on
the promise that their houses would be spared.

The Sultan kept control of some of his regiments to act as his
escort and as military police. But most of his troops were already
eager to begin the looting. The sailors were especially impatient,
fearing that the soldiers would forestall them. Hoping that the
boom would prevent the Christian ships from escaping out of the
harbour and that they could capture them at their leisure they
abandoned their ships to scramble ashore. Their greed saved many
Christian lives. While a number of the Greek and Italian sailors,
including Trevisano himself, were captured before they could escape
from the walls, others were able to join the skeleton crews left on
their ships, unimpeded by any Turkish action, and prepare them for
battle, if need be. Others were able to scramble on to the ships
before they sailed, or to swim out to them like the Florentine Tealdi.
When he saw that the city had fallen Alviso Diedo, as commander of
the fleet, sailed over in a small boat to Pera to ask the Genoese
authorities there whether they intended to advise their fellow-
Genoese to stay in the harbour and fight or to make for the open
sea. His Venetian ships, he promised, would co-operate with whatever decision they made. The Podestà of Pera recommended that
an embassy should go to the Sultan to inquire whether he would
let all the ships go free or whether he would risk war with Genoa
and Venice. The suggestion was hardly practicable at such a
moment; but meanwhile the Podestà had locked the gates of Pera,
and Diedo, with whom was the diarist Barbaro, was unable to rejoin
his ships. But the Genoese sailors in the ships anchored below the
walls of Pera made it known that they intended to sail away and
they wished to have the support of the Venetians. On their insistence
Diedo was allowed to leave in his sloop. He made straight for the
boom, which was still closed. Two of his sailors hacked with axes
at the thongs that bound it to the walls of Pera, and it drifted away
on its floats. Signalling to the ships in the harbour to follow him
Diedo sailed through the gap. Seven Genoese ships from Pera sailed

close behind him, and soon afterwards they were joined by most of
the Venetian warships, by four or five of the Emperor's galleys and
by one or two Genoese warships. They had all waited as long as they
dared to pick up refugees who swam out to them; and after they had
passed through the boom the whole flotilla remained for an hour
or so at the entrance to the Bosphorus to see if any more ships
would escape. Then they took advantage of the strong north wind
that was blowing to sail down the Sea of Marmora through the
Dardanelles to freedom.

So many of Hamza Bey's ships had been deserted by his sailors
in their rush for plunder that he was powerless to stop the flight
of Diedo's fleet. With those of his ships that were still manned he
sailed round over the broken boom into the Golden Horn. There
in the harbour he trapped the ships that were left, another four or
five Imperial galleys, two or three Genoese galleys and all the
unarmed Venetian merchantment. Most of them were crowded with
refugees so far beyond their capacity that they would never have
been able to put out to sea. A few small boats still managed to slip
across to Pera. But in the full light of day it was no longer easy
to elude the Turks. By noon the whole harbour and everything in it
were in the hands of the conquerors.

. . . . .

Sultan Mehmet had already known for many hours that the great
city was his. It was at dawn that his men had broken through the
stockade; and soon afterwards, with the waning moon still high
in the sky, he came himself to examine the breach through which
they had entered. But he waited till afternoon before making his
own triumphant entry into the city, when the first excess of massacre and pillage should be over and some sort of order restored.
In the meantime he returned to his tent, where he received delega-
tions of frightened citizens and the Podestà of Pera in person. He
also wished to discover what had been the fate of the Emperor. That
was never clearly known. A story was circulated later round the
Italian colonies in the Levant that two Turkish soldiers who claimed
to have killed Constantine brought a head to the Sultan which
captured courtiers who were present recognized as their master's.
Mehmet set it for a while on a column in the Augustean Forum, then
stuffed it and sent it to be exhibited round the leading courts of
the Islamic world. Writers who were present at the fall of the city
told different stories. Barbaro reported that some claimed to have

seen the Emperor's body among a pile of the slain but that others maintained that it was never found. The Florentine Tetaldi wrote similarly that some said that his head was sliced off and others that he died at the gate after being struck to the ground. Either story could be true, he added; for he certainly died in the crowd, and the Turks decapitated most of the corpses. His devoted friend Phrantzes tried to find out more details; but he only learnt that when the Sultan sent to search for the body a number of corpses and heads were washed in the hope of identifying him. At last a body was found with an eagle embroidered on the socks and stamped on the greaves. It was assumed to be his; and the Sultan gave it to the Greeks for them to bury. Phrantzes himself did not see it, and he was a little doubtful whether it was really his master's; nor could he find out where it was buried. In later centuries a nameless grave in the Vefa quarter was shown to the pious as the Emperor's burial-place. Its authenticity was never proved, and it is now neglected and forgotten.

Whatever the details may have been, Sultan Mehmet was satisfied that the Emperor was dead. He was now not only Sultan but heir and possessor of the ancient Roman Empire.

5 FROM   *Peter E. Russell*
PRINCE HENRY THE NAVIGATOR

*We are so accustomed to viewing in a commercial perspective the Portugese move-
ment down the coast of West Africa, which carried its mariners eventually to India,
that it may come as a surprise to some that its beginnings were anything but economic in origin. The following sketch makes it clear that Prince Henry the Navigator
was motivated primarily by medieval dreams of crusading and chivalry. His efforts
belong primarily to the medieval era rather than to the Renaissance. His story is
another chapter in the Moslem–Christian conflict of the later middle ages.*

In 1457, in a document issued by his chancery, we find Prince
Henry the Navigator writing . . . in these terms:

"Knowing how, within the memory of men, there was no information among Christians about the seas, lands, and people
beyond Cape Nun towards the south . . . I set about enquiring and
discovering, from many years past to the present time, what lay
from the said Cape Nun onwards, not without great efforts by me
and endless expenses . . . sending during this time many ships and
caravels with my dependants and servants who, by God's grace,
passed beyond the said Cape. . . ."

. . . . .

I do not think it unduly far-fetched to suggest that there is a
certain parallel between the prince's part in the rounding of Cape
Bojador and the preparations which are today being made for men
to travel in still more alarming regions. As in the case of the poli-
ticians, physicists, engineers and psychologists involved in current
space projects, there never seems to have been any question of
Prince Henry himself actually going on any of the voyages made in
his name. This should cause us no surprise; indeed, it is a point
which arises only because, as I have mentioned, English-speaking
writers have bestowed on the prince the ambiguous title of "the

SOURCE. Peter E. Russell, *Prince Henry the Navigator* (London: Hispanic and Luso
Brazilian Councils, 1960), pp. 13–30. Reprinted by permission of the publisher and
the author.

Navigator." Medieval protocol and custom made it unthinkable for a royal prince to sail on voyages of discovery, especially in tiny vessels such as the Portuguese used. His task was to provide ships, the finance, the information, and the psychological preparation needed to make it possible for his pilots, captains and seamen to carry out his plans.

What, however, were the motives behind these plans? This seems to me to be the really important question we have to ask ourselves about Prince Henry.

. . . . .

I have already mentioned that contemporary Portuguese documents describing the prince's discoveries nearly always associate these with crusading or missionary ends. We saw, however, that—since these documents are concerned either with obtaining privileges for Prince Henry or with justifying his use of the revenues of the Order of Christ—it could be held that such an association was made with an ulterior motive. There is, however, one piece of writing which can safely be attributed to the prince himself and which does, undoubtedly, contain a sincere statement of his views about religion, chivalry, and the doctrine of the crusade. Unlike his brothers, King Duarte and the Regent Dom Pedro, or his nephew, King Alfonso, Henry did not leave any literary works behind him. But he did, when at Estremoz in 1436, write a memorial giving his reasons for supporting the much-debated project for a Portuguese attack on Tangier. It is not a very well-argued or even well-written paper.

He begins by observing that the accepted aims of this life are to save one's soul and the honour of one's person, name, lineage, and country, to make the body joyful and, in last place, to achieve temporal gains. He then goes on to stress the supreme importance of honour, and to state his own contempt for the physical pleasures such as eating, drinking, sleeping, singing and the company of women. From this he concludes—somewhat erratically—that the only permissible purpose of life is to serve God and achieve honour. War against the Moors will satisfy both purposes and should, therefore, be undertaken. Since God may be expected to help the Portuguese the king should not fear its outcome. The memorial ends with an encouraging assessment of the supposed military weakness of the kingdom of Fex which, in the event, was to be revealed as wholly erroneous.

Now the Prince Henry who reveals the workings of his mind here is about as far away as possible from the nineteenth-century concept of him as humanist and scientist. He sounds like a character out of a medieval romance of chivalry, not like a field commander staking a claim to be charged with the task of invading a dangerous shore. One is reminded of another aspect of the prince's life which also belongs to the world of romance. I refer to his supposed life-long cult of perfect chastity which three writers who knew him— Zurara, Cà de Mosto and Diogo Gomes—all refer to with undisguised admiration. Whether they spoke the truth or merely sought to flatter him we cannot tell. Obviously there is a possible problem here which deserves greater attention than I can give it. But I think it significant of Prince Henry's exaltation of medieval chivalric ideals that he wished to be remembered for his exceptional chastity.

. . . . .

Zurara [Prince Henry's biographer] gives six reasons for his patron's interest in the discovery of Guinea and the Atlantic Islands. He recognizes, first, that the prince was moved by a desire to find out what lay beyond Cape Bojador in order to open an unknown sea passage to mariners and merchants. But he immediately follows this up with four more reasons, all of which are concerned, in one way or another, with showing that the prince's main concern was with the crusade against the Moors in Africa and with the discovery of infidel souls which might be converted. Zurara ends by explaining that there was one other explanation for the discoveries more powerful than any of these. This was Prince Henry's horoscope. The chronicler describes it in detail and—as far as I can judge— correctly, and then notes that it showed the prince to be predestined to work to achieve great and noble conquests, especially by seeking out secret things hidden from other men.

Zurara's suggestion that astrological prediction influenced Prince Henry's career more than anything else usually gets scant attention from the students of his life. This may well be a mistake. Credence in astrology and horoscopes was general in Europe at this time, and nowhere more so than at the courts of kings and princes. Henry's father, John I, was interested in astrology. His brother, King Duarte, also concerned himself with it. Medieval science was, indeed, completely mixed up with astrology—few branches of it more so than navigation, about which the prince clearly knew something—even if the extent of his knowledge has possibly been somewhat exaggerated. I think it very likely, therefore, that what Zurara has to say on this matter, too, may faithfully reflect Prince Henry's own beliefs about his destiny. The predictions of his horoscope may explain, perhaps, not only why he was always ready to abandon West African exploration for chivalric and crusading adventures in Morocco, and *vice versa*, but also why, for a considerable period, he insisted—otherwise inexplicably—on treating the discovery of Guinea itself as if it were also a war of conquest against the Moors.

Mr. E. W. Bovill discounts the sincerity of the claims of Prince Henry and his seamen that the discovery of Guinea was carried on for missionary purposes. "Their real purpose," he writes, "was not, as they pretended, to spread the Gospel, but to discover the source of the gold which was being imported into Morocco overland by the Taghaza road." The observation may well be true of many of those who—especially after 1443—took part in the African voyages. But, as far as Henry himself is concerned, the suggestion that he was hypocritical is, I think, impossible to sustain. It was clearly not hypocrisy which led him to abandon temporarily the work of discovery and hurl himself into the disaster at Tangier. We may disregard Zurara's evidence on the question of motive as possibly suspect. The constant assertion of a crusading and missionary purpose in contemporary documents may, too, be explained away as belonging to the conventions of self-interest. But there remains what Cà da Mosto has to say. This Venetian captain knew the prince personally and made two voyages to Guinea under his direction in 1455 and 1456. He himself had, as his account of his journeys shows, no particular interest in crusading or in missionary work. Cà da Mosto declares, however, that the prince's wish to discover the African coast was connected with his desire to attack the Moors and refers, also, to the prince's desire to make converts.

. . . . .

It would be difficult to maintain that Prince Henry did not see, in the gold of Guinea, a way by which his own fortunes and those of his country might be saved. This is not merely a matter of deduction. Diogo Gomes, one of his captains, declared categorically of him that—when the prince began his explorations in West Africa— he wished to make contact with the lands from which West African gold reached the north "in order to trade with them and to sustain the nobles of his household."

There was, in principle, no contradiction between the prince's crusading interests and his search for gold. It was proper to deny to the infidel, if possible, one of the sources of his military strength and use it to finance expeditions against him. No one had ever sought to maintain, either, that a crusader might not make as much profit as he could from his crusading—provided he did not forget that his main duty was to wage religious war. The late medieval code of chivalry—as set out, for example, in the *Siete Partidas* of Alfonso the Wise—had, however, added some new complexities to this position. Theoretically at least, any form of buying or selling except in connection with war or the holding of land was considered incompatible with the status of knight. This belief must have caused some difficulty to Prince Henry when it began to look as if he was becoming the leader of an enterprise in which trade, not crusading or conversion of the infidel, was the dominant objective.

It is possible, I think, to see the commercial history of the conquest of Guinea as the story of the way in which the hard realities of economic fact and ordinary human motivation gradually forced themselves into the sublimated world of chivalry and religious zealotry in which the prince sought to live. From the beginning, if Zurara is correct, he openly admitted an intention to trade in Africa, but only if he could find Christian peoples there to trade with. This hope had very soon to be relinquished, because no such peoples were found and trade with the non-Christian inhabitants of Senegambia and the western Sahara became essential if the voyages were to continue. The establishment, in 1443, of Arguin Island as a permanent trading-post for doing business with the Mauretanian Touregs confirms that the pretence of a predominantly crusading objective had already started to break down. Nevertheless, the documents suggest very clearly that the prince was always unwilling fully to accept this situation. He goes on talking—anachronistically—about wars of conquest and the conversion of the natives, even when peaceful trading and the importation of large numbers of slaves purchased by barter from local chiefs had become the order of the day and exploration had largely ceased. Meanwhile the Portuguese merchants and shipowners who, at the beginning, had viewed the prince's high-minded intentions in West Africa with total indifference, now clamoured to have his permission to join him. They were impressed by the sight of the lucrative cargoes of seal-oil, fish, skins, ostrich eggs, sugar from Madeira, dragon's blood and all the other merchandise of Guinea, to say nothing of gold, both yellow and black, which arrived at Lagos and Lisbon in the prince's caravels. After 1446, discovery, as such, takes second place.

We know very little about the exact quantities of gold which reached the homeland after 1441 or 1442, when the first precious dust was brought back. The Portuguese never succeeded in finding the elusive source of West African gold; that secret was kept from Europeans until the time of Mungo Park, though the curiosity and intelligence of Cà da Mosto nearly discovered it when he sailed up the Gambia River in 1456. Gold, however, probably did reach Portugal in sufficient quantities to make a useful contribution to the country's economy. But it was soon found that black gold—slaves—was the most attractive cargo Guinea had to offer. This, it is certain, did make an important contribution to Portuguese economic life by relieving the long-standing and acute shortage of manpower there.

. . . . .

Prince Henry's attitude towards this new trade [in slaves], of which fate had made him the unexpected patron, seems to have been characteristic. Zurar describes his presence on horseback at the 1445 slave-market and clearly finds it embarrassing. The prince, he says, took the customary fifth—forty-six slaves—which belonged to him, but—he hastens to add–showed little interest in the profit to be made from them, preferring instead, "to mediate with great satisfaction on the salvation of those souls which had previously been lost." Certainly, as the documents show, the prince never ceased to justify the development of the slave-trade in terms of conversions. But, by the end of his life, he had evidently come to be rather less contemptuous of the commercial value of African slaves than Zurara would have us believe. In 1457 he ceded to the Order of Christ 1/21 of the value of all merchandise reaching Portugal from the lands over which his commercial monopoly extended. Among the main commodities listed as imported from Guinea he puts—first of all—slaves, male and female, placing them before even gold and fish. They are described as "cousas" (things) just like any other form of merchandise. Yet earlier in the same document, when summarizing his achievements, he had explained how, first by war and then by trade, "a very great number of infidel captives had come to the Christian world, the greater part of whom, offering great praise to Our Lord, have turned to his holy faith; and everything is well-prepared for many more to come." Clearly he found the whole business of his connection with the slave-trade equivocal.

Prince Henry, one may therefore be sure, was never able to disembarrass himself sufficiently of his preconceptions to understand, except dimly and reluctantly, what he had really done. He possessed a variety of commercial monopolies on a great scale, including not only that over all trade with West Africa and the Atlantic Isles, but also over such humdrum things as the fishing rights off the Algarve, the import of dyes and sugar and the control of the soap industry in Portugal. But he remained, it seems, always a *commerçant malgré lui*. Perhaps this was one of the reasons why, despite all the resources he controlled, the prince seems to have lived and died heavily in debt. And the old hankering after great and noble victories against the Moors never ceased to seduce him. In 1458 he succeeded in persuading his nephew and disciple, Alfonso V, to attempt, once again, the conquest of Morocco. Henry, now an old man, did not hesitate, once more, to abandon his West African enterprises in order to take part. Thanks to the prince's obsession the Portuguese were committed to an imperialist programme in North Africa which was, in the end, as the Regent Dom Pedro had predicted, to come near destroying Portuguese independence for good, though that consequence was still far off. Still, it must be remembered when we try to evaluate his achievements.

Our attempt to get at Prince Henry's motives, then, seems to establish two important facts about him and them. His mind was always dominated by a zealous devotion to the twin doctrines of chivalry and crusade. He also exhibited a notable reluctance, or inability, to modify his preconceptions when he was confronted by unforeseen situations—even those which he himself had created. It is important, I think, to note that the doctrines of chivalry and crusade to which he adhered were not Hispanic. In Henry's time the Spaniards were engaged in the penultimate stages of their difficult love-hate relationship with the Moors of Granada. Long practical experience, sometimes painfully acquired, had taught them that their relationship with the Spanish Moors was a subtle and complicated affair. In it, religious zeal and chivalrous idealism had to be tempered by the remembrance of practical realities—especially economic ones. The Portuguese, on the other hand, had no tradition of practical crusading. This was, perhaps, why offers by Prince Henry to join in the war with Granada were politely but firmly turned down by the Castilians. The sort of approach set out in the prince's memorial of 1436 was too Quixotic for them.

. . . . .

I have tried, in this paper, to bring out the importance of medieval crusading and chivalric ideas in Prince Henry's life because, without them, it seems to me that we get nowhere near the man and his motives. For that reason I conclude that the prince belongs essentially to the later Middle Ages, rather than to the humanist and scientific Renaissance, where a long tradition has tended to place him. I think there is much to be said for the conclusion of Dr. Veiga Simões that he was one of the builders of the modern world without intending to be. But if he clung, with characteristic tenacity, to the illusion that his life was dedicated to the crusade and to chivalry we must not forget that it was from this same illusion that he very likely drew the moral strength and the single-mindedness which made it possible for him to carry through the great enterprises of discovery associated with his name. The anachronistic vision of Prince Henry led, past Africa, towards the Indian Ocean and a great commercial empire. Dom Pedro's prudence perhaps would have led to no more than acceptance by the Portuguese of a modest provincial status on the confines of western Europe.

I am reminded of the famous portrait of Henry in the painting (c. 1465) by Nuno Gonçalves. Perhaps it is not really a portrait from life. But Nuno Gonçalves seems, at any rate, to have visualized very exactly the personality of the prince as we may suppose it to have been towards the end of his life. Strength, even rigidity, is there. The expression of the eyes is firmly ultramundane still. But there is also a sense of melancholy and disillusion, not of achievement. One thinks, inevitably, of the parallel with Columbus, another man with a clutter of medieval notions in his mind and an unshakeable sense of mission, who also found a new world which was not the one he expected to find. Who, too, could never quite reconcile himself to accepting what he had found for what it was, rather than what he had wanted it to be. Neither is less great, and certainly not less human, because of this inability to trim his dreams to fit actualities obvious to lesser men. Indeed, when one comes to think about it, it seems certain that both discoverers owed everything to this furrow of Quixotism in their natures.

6 FROM   *Roger B. Merriman*

THE CONQUEST OF GRANADA

The Conquest of Granada, coming as it did on the eve of Columbus' voyage west, has fascinated historians from the time of Washington Irving's early book covering the Fall of Granada, which he wrote after his sojourn in Spain. It does mark the end of one age and the beginning of another. Yet it also has an important place in the history of Moslem—Western Christian relations. By this conquest, in a special way, Christendom made up for the earlier loss of Constantinople and began the conquest of the Atlantic. The end of the last anti-Moslem Crusade inaugurated Western Europe's new destiny on the seven seas of the world.

No more fitting celebration of the union of the Spanish kingdoms could have been imagined than that they should jointly proceed to the completion of the great work of the Reconquest, and round out their dominions by the final expulsion of the Moors from the peninsula.

Since the battle on the Salado in the reign of Alfonso XI, the Christians had scored but three important victories against the forces of the kings of Granada. A great battle had been won by the armies of John II at Sierra Elvira, close to Granada, in 1431; in 1410 and in 1462 the town of Antequera and the Rock of Gibraltar had been captured. During the latter part of the reign of Henry IV and the first five years of that of Ferdinand and Isabella the internal troubles of the realm effectually prevented any renewal of attacks against the Moorish strongholds. When in 1476 the queen sent to demand payment of the annual tribute due from the king of Granada, the latter evinced his contempt of his Christian overlords by the famous answer, that the mints of his realm "coined no longer gold, but steel." Their Catholic Majesties were still too busy with other cares to heed this insolent reply, and their failure promptly to chastise their haughty vassal encouraged him in 1481 to surprise the Christian fortress of Zahara on the confines of the province of

SOURCE. Roger Bigelow Merriman, *The Rise of the Spanish Empire in the Old World and in the New* (New York: The Macmillan Company. Copyright, 1918, by The Macmillan Company; renewed, 1946, by Dorothea F. Merriman), pp. 62–75. Reprinted by permission of the publisher.

Cadiz. But by this time the Christians were in better condition to retaliate. The War of Succession with Portugal had been triumphantly terminated. John of Aragon was dead, and Ferdinand was in full possession of his hereditary domains. A report that the important fortress of Alhama, on a rocky peak in the vega just southwest of Granada, was inadequately garrisoned and negligently guarded, led to the despatch of Rodrigo Ponce de Leon, the fiery Marquis of Cadiz, in February, 1482, on a desperate attempt to seize it unawares. The expedition, which demanded quite as much proficiency in rock climbing as in fighting, was extremely hazardous but completely successful; and the subsequent efforts of the Moors to retake the place were beaten off. From that moment the campaign against Granada ceased to be a mere series of forays, and assumed the character of a regular, methodically conducted war. The sovereigns took it up vigorously, with the idea of ending once and for all the Moorish hold on the peninsula. The Emir, reading the signs of the times, solicited aid from the Merinites across the Strait, but Isabella checkmated this move by sending a Castilian fleet to cruise in the adjacent waters, and to cut off all communication with the African coast.

And now, just at the moment when the Moors of Granada needed all their forces to withstand the Christian attack, they were seriously weakened at home by dynastic quarrels of the typical Mohammedan sort. Jealousies in the harem of the Emir, Abul Hassan, were the source of it; the famous massacre of the Cordovan family of the Abencerrages in the Alhambra and the imprisonment of the queen and her son, Boabdil, were its first results. But the captives contrived to escape from their confinement and to enlist the sympathies of the Granadinos; after a series of bloody feuds the old Emir was expelled, and forced to seek refuge at the court of his brother in Malaga. The latter's energy and bravery had won him the title of El Zagal or "the Valiant," and his prestige reached its climax in the spring of 1483 by his brilliant victory over an expedition which the indefatigable Marquis of Cadiz had led into the neighbouring territories. But the ultimate result of the triumph of El Zagal was distinctly unfavorable to the Moorish cause. It inspired his nephew, Boabdil, to attempt to emulate his exploits; but El Rey Chico, as the Spaniards called him, was proverbially unlucky in everything that he undertook, and instead of eclipsing his uncle's victory, as he had hoped, he was speedily defeated and captured by the Castilian Count of Cabra. A vigorous debate

ensued among the Christian leaders as to the most profitable way to
make use of the prize which fortune had placed in their hands; but
the final verdict was that Boabdil should be released and sent back
to his own dominions, on terms which bound him hand and foot
to the cause of Ferdinand and Isabella, and which consequently
insured the vigorous continuance of the internal quarrels in
Granada. Boabdil did not refuse these degrading conditions. He
sneaked back into his capital, where El Zagal had meantime succeeded in establishing himself; though he failed to gain admittance
to the Alhambra and the upper town, he soon gathered his adherents on the banks of the Darro and the Xenil, and waged a
murderous war upon his rivals. In the midst of the confusion, the
old king, Abul Hassan, disappeared, not improbably a victim of
foul play.

While revolt and sedition were thus rife in the Moorish camp, the
Christian army presented a spectacle of enthusiastic unity and devotion such as Spain had seldom, if ever, witnessed before. A number
of different causes contributed to this happy result. In the first place
every effort was used to make men feel that it was a national
Spanish enterprise—the first of its kind—made possible by the
marriage of Ferdinand and Isabella, and not an affair of merely
local import. As the kingdom of Granada nowhere touched the
realms of the Crown of Aragon, Castile alone could hope to benefit
territorially by its reconquest; nevertheless Ferdinand was fully as
active in the prosecution of the war as was the queen, whose services,
though undoubtedly extraordinary, have probably been somewhat
exaggerated in the gallant phrases of the contemporary chroniclers.
And as the best possible method of stimulating the spirit of unity so
essential to success, the sovereigns did their utmost to instil into
their troops the conviction that the war was rather religious than
political in its aims. They strove their hardest to awaken the old
crusading ardor, which had been dormant for long periods in the
past, but which, when thoroughly roused, had shown itself capable
of working wonders, as in the campaigns of Las Navas and the
Salado. During the year 1486, in the very midst of the struggle, the
king and queen made a solemn pilgrimage to the shrine of Santiago
de Compostela. A huge silver cross, the gift of Pope Sixtus IV, was
carried in Ferdinand's tent throughout the campaign; it was invari-
ably raised by the royal standard bearer on the topmost pinnacle of
each conquered town and adored with impressive ceremonies by the
assembled hosts. Finally, the constant presence of Ferdinand and

Isabella in the midst of their advancing armies was a tremendous asset for the cause. It was the surest possible way of keeping the factious nobles from deserting, of maintaining order and discipline in the ranks, of convincing the soldiers that there was no duty they were called upon to perform in which their sovereigns were too proud to bear a part. And the enthusiasm which the enterprise kindled in Spain extended before long to other lands as well. . . .

. . . . .

The year 1484 was marked by no important event, but in 1485–86 the Christian lines were drawn considerably tighter around the Moorish [kingdom]. The western outpost of Ronda, perched on the summit of a precipitous cliff, succumbed to the artillery of the Marquis of Cadiz. Wedges were driven into the heart of the infidel realm by the capture of Loja and Illora, and the fall of Marbella on the Mediterranean coast afforded an invaluable base of operations for the blockading Castilian fleet. In 1487 everything was concentrated on the siege of Malaga, the largest of the outward defences of the kingdom of Granada, and, with the exception of Almeria, its only remaining seaport of importance. An indispensable preliminary was the capture of Velez, situated on the road from Malaga to Granada; and in April Ferdinand crossed the Sierras with a large army and finally sat down before its walls. El Zagal sallied forth from Granada in a desperate effort to relieve it, but was unsuccessful; moreover his treacherous nephew seized the opportunity to make himself supreme within the capital, which shut its gates on El Zagal when he attempted to return thither after his failure, and finally obliged him to seek refuge in the eastern cities of Guadix, Baza, and Almeria, the only portions of the realm which remained loyal to him. Meantime Velez surrendered, and the blockade of Malaga began. It was a long and arduous undertaking. The garrison was largely composed of African troops, who had more stomach for fighting than the Spanish Moors; the fortifications were very strong, and high hopes were entertained of relief from the Barbary coast. But the vigilance of the Castilian fleet prevented that, while the wretched Boabdil attacked and cut to pieces a rescuing party despatched by his uncle, El Zagal; on the other hand the arrival of Queen Isabella in the camp of the besiegers redoubled their enthusiasm, and imbued them with a chivalrous resolve to do or die for the cause. Sudden assaults by the Christians and sorties by their foes varied the monotony of the blockade; but the crucial event of the entire siege was the effort of a Moorish fanatic, who had gained access to the royal tent on the plea that he was inspired with the gift of prophecy, to assassinate the king and queen. Happily the attempt failed, but the news that the lives of their sovereigns had been imperilled served to rouse the loyalty and ardor of the Christians to the highest pitch. Everything was got ready for a grand assault, which, however, was delayed for a brief period owing to Isabella's desire to save bloodshed; meantime the spectacle of the besiegers' preparations, coupled with the terrible dearth of provisions within the town, convinced the defenders that there was no alternative to an acknowledgment of defeat. After a fruitless effort to extort lenient conditions from Ferdinand by a threat of massacring the five or six hundred Christian captives in the dungeons of Malaga, the inhabitants surrendered at discretion. Whether owing to the fact that the garrison was largely composed of African troops, or to some other cause, does not appear; but it is certain that the terms which Ferdinand imposed on the conquered town form a most disagreeable contrast to those granted to the places which he had captured before. The whole population was virtually condemned to slavery. One third was transported to North Africa to be exchanged for Christian captives there detained; another was appropriated by the state as payment for the expenses of the campaign; the rest were distributed among the nobles, the Pope, and the sovereigns of friendly lands. One hundred warriors were incorporated into the papal guard and converted, before the year was out, into "very good Christians"; fifty beautiful damsels were presented to the queen of Naples, and thirty to the queen of Portugal. Such was the perhaps not entirely unmerited revenge for the hosts of Christian maidens, seized in Spain during the previous seven centuries and despatched across the dreary wastes of Northern Africa to supply the harems of the Orient.

The fall of Malaga rendered that of Granada ultimately inevitable. But Ferdinand and Isabella were resolved to take no chances, and in order to make assurance doubly sure, directed all their energies during the years 1488 and 1489 to the reduction of that eastern extremity of the Moorish territories which acknowledged the sway of El Zagal. In 1488 Ferdinand advanced along the coast to attack Almeria, only to be beaten off with heavy loss by his crafty opponent. In 1489 the Christians centred their efforts on the siege of Baza with better success. The town finally surrendered, after prolonged resistance, at the very end of the year. As Boabdil did nothing to help his uncle, the latter recognized the necessity of admitting defeat. Negotiations and a personal interview with Ferdinand followed, and finally ended in an arrangement by which the Moorish king surrendered to the Christians all the principal fortresses of the realm, including Guadix and Almeria, and received in return the sovereignty of the small district southwest of Malaga, to be held by him as a vassal of the king of Castile. But El Zagal was much too proud to be permanently satisfied with so shadowy a vestige of royalty. He soon disposed of his new dominions to the king and queen of Castile in return for a money indemnity, and passed over to Africa, where, stripped of everything by the savage Berbers, he ended his days in misery and solitude. He was by far the ablest figure on the Moorish side of this last great contest of Cross and Crescent in the peninsula, and assuredly deserved a better fate.

Meantime the unhappy Boabdil, whose treachery was only equalled by his ineptitude, seized the moment of his uncle's defeat to renounce the obligations to the king and queen of Castile which he had contracted at the time of his capture, and hurled defiance at Ferdinand and Isabella. In the spring of 1490 the Christian armies camped on the broad vega beneath Granada. The troops were in splendid condition; everything combined to make them certain of victory, and yet they did not underestimate the difficulties of the crowning task. With a full realization that time was indispensable to success, and a permanent fortified base on the vega the best guarantee for the maintenance of a rigid blockade, they constructed, during the winter of 1490–91, a new town in the wide plain, six miles to the west of Granada, and significantly named it Santa Fé. It was laid out in the form of a Roman camp, with regular streets crossing each other at right angles—"the only city in Spain that has never been contaminated by the Moslem heresy"; it was destined to be the scene of the capitulation of Granada, and of the signing of the contract with Columbus which led to the discovery of a New World. The sight of such a formidable establishment was profoundly discouraging to the beleaguered Moors. It proved to them that their foes would never cease from their efforts until their object had been triumphantly accomplished; and in October, 1491, negotiations for the surrender of Granada were begun, Hernando de Zafra, the royal secretary, and Gonsalvo de Cordova being entrusted with the conduct of them on the Christian side. After long conferences the terms were finally settled on the twenty-fifth of the following November; they were exceedingly liberal—the sharpest possible contrast to the vengeance that had been visited upon Malaga. The city was to be surrendered within sixty days, and the artillery and fortifications given up. The Moors, however, were to be permitted to retain unmolested their customs, dress, property, laws, and religion; they were to continue to be ruled by their own local magistrates, under the supervision of a governor appointed by the Castilian crown. They were carefully guarded against extortionate taxes, and they were to be furnished transportation to North Africa in case they desired to emigrate. The conditions, indeed, were in general such as did high honor to the magnanimity and generosity of the victors, and rendered the subsequent violation of them the more shameful. The actual surrender took place with impressive ceremonies on January 2, 1492. Pradilla's great painting accurately depicts the scene as the contemporary chroniclers have described it —the stately courtesy of Ferdinand and Isabella, the timorous hesitancy of the vanquished Boabdil.

> *Here passed away the Koran ; there in the Cross was borne ;*
> *And here was heard the Christian bell ; and there the Moorish horn.*

It was indeed a glorious victory, won at a critical moment, and stained by few acts of treachery and cruelty. It had evoked all that was best in the character of the Spaniard. It showed that under the inspiration of a Holy War, hallowed by nearly eight centuries of national tradition, he could rise superior to petty local aims and ambitions, and was capable of really great things. It served, as perhaps nothing else could have done, to win enthusiastic support for the throne of Ferdinand and Isabella, by identifying their rule at the very outset with the advancement of the Faith, and with the successful completion of the national task. But there is grave danger in regarding the conquest of Granada merely as marking the end of an epoch. In many ways it was not so much an end as a beginning. We have already observed that no sharp dividing line can be drawn between reconquest and conquest; the two merge into one another and form a continuous whole. Attempts had been made to secure a footing in North Africa for centuries before Granada fell; and a year after its surrender Ferdinand and Isabella despatched a certain Lorenzo de Padilla, governor of Alcalá, in disguise to the Barbary coast, to gather information which should be valuable to them in the event of their carrying their arms across the Strait. Clearly the Catholic Kings had already made up their minds to pursue the Crescent beyond the borders of Spain. Moreover, it so

happened that in the midst of all these exciting events a very persistent Italian mariner, whom many men thought to be half mad,
but whom the sovereigns believed in and supported, came back
from a long voyage of discovery into the West, with marvellous tales
of new lands to conquer beyond the seas. Everything combined to
beckon the new monarchs forward and onward at this crucial stage
in their career. Certainly it was no time for them to rest on their
laurels.

But internal reforms of the most drastic and far reaching sort
were the indispensable preliminary to foreign conquest. They had
indeed been largely accomplished during the period of the
Granadan war, and we must study them carefully before turning to
the story of Spain's new career of expansion beyond the seas.

EPILOGUE

By the time Columbus had laid the foundations of Spain's New World Empire and Vasco de Gama had reached the shores of South India, the hostility and divergence between Western Europeans and Moslems had become so intense that they fought continuously for the next century and a half. In the Mediterranean, Turkish and corsair fleets battled Spanish, Genoese, and Venetian flotillas for mastery, while each side periodically raided its opponent's shores. In the Indian Ocean, Western warships, first Portuguese and then Dutch, swept the seas clear of organized Moslem fleets and diverted local commerce and long-distance traffic alike into European vessels.

By 1650 the results of these conflicts had become momentous for Islamic civilization in general. Moslem north Africa became economically impoverished as the trans-Saharan traffic, which had sustained it, was diverted to European vessels operating along the Atlantic coast of West Africa. Piracy was almost the only profitable activity remaining for North Africa to pursue. And piracy was as disorganizing to North African social life as the steady encroachment of desert tribesmen on its settled agricultural areas. Along the east coast of Africa, most Islamic cities simply disappeared, while Moslem shippers of the Red Sea, Persian Gulf, and Hadramaut were reduced to an unimportant traffic along East African shores and across the Indian Ocean to India and Ceylon.

While Moslem power was fading along the shores of the Eastern Mediterranean, the long duel between Ottomans on the one hand and Spanish and Italians on the other ended, by the mid-seventeenth century, with both sides impoverished and nomadism increasingly prevalent in areas of Egypt, Syria, and Asia Minor where it had been unknown earlier. In Central and

Eastern Europe also, the long war between Hapsburg and Turk tragically delayed the development of Hungarians, Western Slavs, Rumanians, and Russians. Only in Moghul India and for brief periods in parts of the Ottoman Empire and Saffavid Persia do we find a vigorous economic and cultural life still in existence during this period, and even this did not last into the eighteenth century.

Islamic civilization, thanks to its hostility toward the West and its growing economic impoverishment, was thus shut off from the changes which were transforming Western Europe during the early modern period. It clung to its increasingly fossilized religious ideals and practices, to a government by military élites often composed of alien slave or renegade warriors, and to a traditional type of literature and art more and more incapable of creative innovation. Only perhaps in Moghul India did it show an ability to absorb new and alien ideas—in this case mainly in the spheres of art and architecture. By the eighteenth century it had relapsed into an age marked by hostility to most manifestations of Western civilization—from which it was not to emerge until the nineteenth and twentieth centuries. This was the tragic heritage of Islamic and Western contacts during the Middle Ages.